CW00969124

ESSENTIAL
IBIZA & FORMENTERA

Original text by Richard Sale
Revised and updated by James Stewart

© AA Media Limited 2010
First published 2008. Revised 2010

ISBN 978-0-7495-6675-3

Published by AA Publishing, a trading name of AA Media Limited, whose registered office is Fanum House, Basing View, Basingstoke, Hampshire RG21 4EA. Registered number 06112600.

Colour separation by AA Digital Department
Printed and bound in Italy by Printer Trento S.r.l.

A04192
Maps in this title produced from mapping © MAIRDUMONT/Falk Verlag 2010

About this book

Symbols are used to denote the following categories:

➕ map reference to maps on cover

✉ address or location

☎ telephone number

🕐 opening times

💷 admission charge

🍴 restaurant or café on premises
   or nearby

🚊 nearest underground train station

🚍 nearest bus/tram route

🚆 nearest overground train station

⛴ nearest ferry stop

✈ nearest airport

❓ other practical information

ℹ tourist information office

➤ indicates the page where you will
   find a fuller description

This book is divided into five sections:

The essence of Ibiza and Formentera
pages 6–19
Introduction; Features; Food and drink;
Short break

Planning pages 20–33
Before you go; Getting there; Getting
around; Being there

Best places to see pages 34–55
The unmissable highlights of any visit
to Ibiza and Formentera

Best things to do pages 56–71
Great places to have lunch; best
beaches; great clubs; markets; stunning
views and more

Exploring pages 72–153
The best places to visit in Ibiza and
Formentera, organized by area

Maps
All map references are to the maps on
the covers. For example, Cala d'Hort has
the reference ➕ 2C – indicating the
grid square in which it is to be found

Admission prices
Inexpensive (under €2)
Moderate (€2–€4)
Expensive (over €4)

Hotel prices
Price is per double room, per night:
€ budget (under €90)
€€ moderate (€90–€160)
€€€ expensive (over €160)

Restaurant prices
Price for a three-course meal per person
without drinks:
€ budget (under €20)
€€ moderate (€20–€40)
€€€ expensive (over €40)

3

Contents

BEST THINGS TO DO

56 – 71

EXPLORING...

72 – 153

The
essence
of. . .

Ibiza is an island that somehow manages to captivate and accommodate legions of clubbers, bohemian travellers, a gay village and masses of holidaymakers. It's a uniquely open-minded place, which becomes the epicentre of the global club scene in the summer months, but still has dozens of undeveloped cove beaches, wildly beautiful landscapes and unspoiled inland villages where life revolves around the traditions of the countryside, not the rhythms of the dance floor.

Formentera, a short ferry ride to the south, is very different, a laidback island of white sandy beaches and lonely hamlets with an unhurried charm.

features

IBIZA

- Area: 570sq km (220sq miles).
- Highest point: Sa Talaia, at 475m (1,558ft).
- Longest river: Riu de Santa Eulària. The river is 11km (7 miles) long and is the only river in the Balearic Islands. Santa Eulària des Riu is therefore the only Balearic town that stands on a river.
- Length of coastline: 210km (130 miles).
- Population: about 133,000, of whom nearly 47,000 live in Eivissa.
- Ibiza lies about 80km (50 miles) from mainland Spain.

FORMENTERA

- Area: 80sq km (31sq miles).
- Highest point: La Mola at 192m (630ft).
- Length: Formentera is only 19km (12 miles) from end to end.
- Population: about 9,000.
- Formentera lies about 220km (137 miles) from North Africa.

CLIMATE
● On average, Ibiza and Formentera have 300 days of sunshine each year. In summer there is an average of 10 hours' sunshine every day.
● Ibiza and Formentera enjoy a typically Mediterranean climate, with hot summers and mild winters.

FAMOUS FOR:
● Tourism. In summer there are four tourists for every native islander.
● Hippies. Thousands came here in the 1960s, and many never left.
● Nude bathing, which is practised with enthusiasm on many beaches.
● Clubbing. Ibiza has seven colossal, cutting-edge venues.
● Potteries. On Formentera look for pieces bearing a lizard motif.
● Leatherware, a traditional craft.
● Art galleries, because the light and climate attract artists.
● Ad Lib fashion, characterized by flowing white linen dresses.

HEDONISM
● Clubbing: Ibiza is the epicentre of global club culture in the summer.
● Accommodation: choose a stylish rural hotel.
● Dining: eat at a superb beach restaurant.
● Drinks: enjoy the vibrant bar scene.

THE ESSENCE OF IBIZA & FORMENTERA

food & drink

The cuisine of the islands reflects both their varied history and the impact of mass tourism on them. Spanish specialities, particularly fish and meat dishes and tapas menus, are usually excellent, but you'll also find a cosmopolitan choice of international cuisine: sushi bars, authentic pizzerias and several Thai restaurants.

IBIZAN AND FORMENTERAN CUISINE

Local cuisine is strongly influenced by the mainland, and most menus specialize in prime fillets of meat and fish, lightly seasoned and perfectly grilled, with a few vegetables on the side. In Ibiza and Formentera the emphasis is on the quality and freshness of the ingredients, so fancy sauces and elaborately presented dishes are not common.

Local specialities are often tricky to find. Rich meat stews like *sofrit pagès* (with lamb and chicken) are delicious, and often feature in winter at traditional countryside restaurants. In summer, however, they are heavy on the stomach. Look, too, for *sobrassada* and *butifarra* sausages, made from coarsely minced pork and spices. The local version of

paella, *arròsec*, has meat (usually rabbit) and vegetables, while *arròs amb peix* includes fish and shellfish.

Good fish soups include *bullit de peix*, or *sopa de rap*, which is made with monkfish. *Guisat de peix* is a fish-based stew, while *guisat de marisc* is similar, but chiefly uses shellfish.

FISH SPECIALITIES

It's worth remembering that there are only a dozen or so fish native to the southern Balearics, so sea bass, salmon and sole are all imported. Locals prize *gall* (John Dory), *raor* (wrasse), *moll roquer* (red mullet) and *mero* (grouper) above all else,

though *dorada* (gildhead bream) is more affordable as it is farmed in Spain. *Tonyina al Eivissenca* is a particular Ibizan tuna dish, the fish being served in a sauce of pine nuts, eggs and white wine.

DESSERTS

For dessert, try *ensaimada*, the typical Ibizan cake of a light pastry filled with cream or almond paste and sprinkled with sugar *(ensaimadas* are also served at breakfast), *orietas*, an aniseed cake, or *flaó*, a cheesecake flavoured with mint. *Flaó* is believed to be Carthaginian in origin.

WINES AND SPIRITS

Spain produces some excellent wines, but local conditions are not ideal for cultivation and there are only three commercial vineyards in Ibiza; Can Maymo near Sant Mateu produces a decent, robust red and a white. It's easy to get a very drinkable bottle in a restaurant for under €12; the Spanish regions of

Navarra, Rioja and Ribero del Duero are the most reliable, and best represented.

Sangria is famous throughout Spain. As elsewhere, island *sangria* is a mixture of red wine, brandy, mineral water and fruit juice, served iced: depending on the mixture, it can have quite a kick.

The islands are famous for their herb spirits. *Hierbas* is herb-based – usually thyme, known locally as *frigola*, although other herbs are used occasionally – and flavoured with aniseed. Many of the local bars blend their own versions of *hierbas*. If you want to try some, look out for a bottle stuffed with twigs of thyme, and ask for a *chupito* (shot).

short break

If you have only a short time to visit Ibiza and Formentera and would like to take home some unforgettable memories, you can do something local and capture the real flavour of the islands. The following suggestions cover a range of sights and experiences that won't take very long, won't cost very much and will make your visit special.

- **Take a walk around Dalt Vila** (➤ 40–41), Eivissa's historic walled enclave, with museums, town houses, cobbled lanes, a cathedral and castle.
- **Find a quiet section of coast** and go for a walk. Northwest Ibiza rewards with stunning sea cliffs. Near Cap de Barbària, on Formentera, you can gaze out across the Mediterranean towards Africa.

- **Take a boat trip** to Formentera if you are based on Ibiza. The main resorts offer day trips (➤ 27).
- **Explore an inland village** on Ibiza. Prosperous Santa Gertrudis is a great choice, with its many cafés and restaurants. On Formentera, Sant Francesc is atmospheric and architecturally interesting.
- **Join in a *ball pagè*,** the traditional island festival with music and singing; discover that the locals do occasionally let their hair down.

● **Go for a swim.** No visit is complete without a dip in the clear, warm waters. To swim in style, take off your clothes at one of the official nudist beaches. In Formentera nudism is permitted on most beaches; in Ibiza it is allowed at Es Cavallet and Aigües Blanques and is acceptable at remote rocky coves.

● **Eat fresh fish** at a *chiringuito* (beach restaurant). Some of the islands' most enjoyable seafood places resemble humble shacks on the beach.

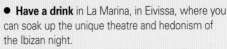

- **Have a drink** in La Marina, in Eivissa, where you can soak up the unique theatre and hedonism of the Ibizan night.
- **Go clubbing:** join the international jet set, fashionistas and the world's best DJs, who transform Ibiza into the planet's clubbing capital in summer. The only decision is which club to choose.

- **On your last night** take a glass of *sangria* to a cliff top on the western side of the island and watch the sun setting over the Mediterranean.

Planning

Before you go

WHEN TO GO

JAN	FEB	MAR	APR	MAY	JUN	JUL	AUG	SEP	OCT	NOV	DEC
14°C	14°C	16°C	19°C	22°C	26°C	28°C	29°C	27°C	23°C	19°C	16°C
57°F	57°F	61°F	66°F	72°F	79°F	82°F	84°F	81°F	73°F	66°F	61°F

High season Low season

Temperatures are the average daily maximum for each month. Ibiza and Formentera operate on a six-month tourist season, which begins on 1 May and finishes on 31 October. The high season runs from July through to early September, when the islands are at their most crowded. June is usually wonderful, while the sea remains warm until late October. Winter is a superb time to visit; though the climate is less reliable, it's very rarely chilly, with clear blue skies and mild evenings usually the norm. The problem is getting to the islands – direct flights from the UK operate only a few times a week between November and April, so you may have to travel via another city in Spain. Many smaller resorts close down for winter, but there is still plenty of accommodation in Eivissa and Sant Antoni. If you're a hiker or a biker it's the perfect time of year for exploration.

WHAT YOU NEED

		UK	Germany	USA	Netherlands	Spain
●	Required	Some countries require a passport to remain valid for a minimum period (usually at least six months) beyond the date of entry – contact their consulate or embassy or your travel agency for details.				
○	Suggested					
▲	Not required					

	UK	Germany	USA	Netherlands	Spain
Passport	●	●	●	●	●
Visa (regulations can change – check before booking your trip)	▲	▲	▲	▲	▲
Onward or return ticket	○	○	○	○	○
Health inoculations	▲	▲	▲	▲	▲
Health documentation (➤ 23, Health Insurance)	●	●	●	●	▲
Travel insurance	○	○	○	○	○
Driving licence (national with Spanish translation or international)	●	●	●	●	●
Car insurance certificate (if own car)	●	●	●	●	●
Car registration document (if own car)	●	●	●	●	●

WEBSITES

www.ibiza.travel
(official tourism website)
www.ibiza-spotlight.com
(best all-round site)
www.ibiza-voice.com
(specializes in club culture)

www.theibizasun.com
(weekly news round-up)
www.liveibiza.com
(historical and cultural resource)
www.guiaformentera.com
(good Formenteran information)

TOURIST OFFICES AT HOME

In the UK
Spanish Tourist Office
79 New Cavendish
Street, London
W1W 6XB
☎ 020 7486 8077
www.spain.info

In the USA
Tourist Office of Spain
666 Fifth Avenue
35th Floor, New York
NY 10103
☎ 212/265-8822
www.okspain.org

Tourist Office of Spain
8383 Wilshire Boulevard
Suite 960
Beverly Hills
CA 90211
☎ 323/658-7195
www.okspain.org

HEALTH INSURANCE

EU nationals can get reduced-cost medical treatment with the relevant documentation (EHIC – European Health Insurance Card), although private medical insurance is still advised and is essential for all other visitors. US visitors should check their insurance coverage.

   Dental treatment is not usually available free of charge as all dentists practise privately. A list of *dentistas* can be found in the yellow pages of the telephone directory. Dental treatment should be covered by private medical insurance.

TIME DIFFERENCES

GMT	Ibiza	Germany	USA (NY)	Netherlands	Italy
12 noon	→ 1PM	→ 1PM	← 7AM	→ 1PM	→ 1PM

Like the rest of Spain, Ibiza and Formentera are one hour ahead of Greenwich Mean Time (GMT+1), but from late March until October summer time (GMT+2) operates.

NATIONAL HOLIDAYS

1 Jan *New Year's Day*	May/June *Corpus Christi*	1 Nov *All Saints' Day*
6 Jan *Epiphany*	25 Jul *St James' Day*	6 Dec *Constitution Day*
Mar/Apr *Good Friday, Easter Monday*	15 Aug *Assumption of the Virgin*	8 Dec *Feast of the Immaculate Conception*
1 May *Labour Day*	12 Oct *National Day*	25 Dec *Christmas Day*

WHAT'S ON WHEN

17 January *Festival of Sant Antoni* in the town of Sant Antoni on Ibiza.

February Carnival season on Ibiza. The main event is on 12 February at Santa Eulària.

Easter *Processions* on Good Friday and Easter Sunday.

First Sunday in May *Procession* of decorated wagons in Santa Eulària, plus classical music concerts.

30 May *Festival of Sant Ferran* in the village of the saint's name in Formentera.

23/24 June *Festival of Sant Joan*, with bonfires and fireworks at many locations. One of the best festivals is at La Mola, Formentera, with a bonfire kept alight throughout the year's shortest night.

16 July *Festival of Verge del Carmen*
(Our Lady of Carmen). The Virgin is the patron saint of seafarers. Parades of boats on Ibiza (particularly in Eivissa's harbour) and Formentera (at La Savina). At the end of the procession the boats are blessed on the water.

25 July *Festival of Sant Jaume*, the patron saint of Formentera. Festivals around the island. The celebrations last for several days and include traditional *ball pagès* (► 17).

5 August *Festival of Our Lady of the Snows*, the patron saint of Ibiza, including a special service in the cathedral.

6 August As part of the *Festival of Our Lady of the Snows* Ibiza's corsairs are honoured with celebrations in Eivissa's harbour.

8 August *Festival of Sant Ciriac.* The Christian Reconquest of the island is celebrated with fireworks and a watermelon fight outside the walls of Dalt Vila.

24 August *Festival in Sant Antoni.* Bands and fireworks celebrate Sant Bartolomeu's Day.

8 September *Fiesta de Jesús.* Religious but with traditional song and dance.

29 September *Festival of St Michael* at Sant Miquel. Folk dancing and traditional music.

12 October *El Pilar,* Formentera. Formal procession to the highest point on the island in honour of Our Lady of El Pilar.

1 November *All Saints' Day* celebrations on Ibiza and Formentera. Baking and eating cakes.

3 December *Bonfire and barbecue* of pig meat in Plaça de la Església, Sant Francesc de Formentera, to celebrate the patron saint's day.

Getting there

BY AIR

Ibiza (Es Codolar) Airport

10km (6 miles) to Eivissa centre

🚇 N/A

🚌 15 minutes

🚗 10 minutes

Ibiza's modern airport (☎ 971 80 90 00) is 10km (6 miles) south of the centre of Eivissa, connected by a fast highway. Buses link the airport with Eivissa (Jul, Aug 7am–5:30am; May, Jun, Sep, Oct 6am–midnight; Nov–Apr 7am–11pm), Sant Antoni (Jun–Sep 7:30am–midnight) and Santa Eulària (Jun–Sep 7:30am–9pm).

BY FERRY

There are ferry services from the Spanish mainland to Ibiza. Formentera does not have an airport and can be accessed only by ferry from Ibiza.

Getting around

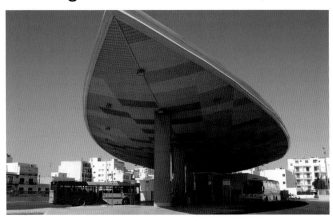

PUBLIC TRANSPORT

Internal flights Several airlines offer flights from Ibiza to Mallorca and to cities on the mainland, including Madrid, Barcelona and Valencia. Airlines include Iberia (☎ 902 400 500; www.iberia.com), Spanair (☎ 902 13 14 15; www.spanair.com) and Vueling (☎ 807 200 200; www.vueling.com).

Buses In Ibiza there is a good service between Eivissa, Sant Antoni and Santa Eulària (every 15–30 minutes) and also buses to many popular beaches, including Portinatx, Cala Tarida, Port de Sant Miquel and Cala Vedella; for all schedules consult www.ibizabus.com or pick up leaflets from tourist offices (➤ 29). In Formentera, buses are less frequent and only connect settlements along the main island road, plus a couple of resort zones. The tourist office can provide a timetable.

Ferries Formentera can be reached by ferry (1 hour) or hydrofoil (35 minutes) from Eivissa. All boats leave from the harbourfront on Avinguda Santa Eulària. During the summer, boats leave every 30 minutes or so, but between November and April there are only five daily sailings. Tourist boats leave in summer from Sant Antoni, Santa Eulària and Es Canar.

TAXIS

All taxis have meters, and fares are pretty reasonable – from the airport to Eivissa is about €12, while Santa Eulària to Sant Antoni is around €24. Prices rise by a few euros at night. There are ranks in all the main towns, or you can phone for a taxi (Eivissa ☎ 971 39 84 83; Santa Eulària ☎ 971 33 33 33; Sant Antoni ☎ 971 34 37 64). Taxis are cheap in Formentera; there are ranks at La Savina, Sant Francesc (☎ 971 32 20 16) and Es Pujols.

FARES AND TICKETS

Return boat tickets to Formentera cost between €28 and €39 for foot passengers and from €90 for cars. Senior citizens qualify for a discount on ferry services. Bus services cost €1–€2.90, depending on the distance.

DRIVING
- There are no motorways on Ibiza or Formentera.
- Speed limits on main roads: 100kph (62mph)
  Speed limits on minor roads: 90kph (56mph)
  Speed limits on urban roads: 50kph (31mph)
- Seat belts must be worn in front seats at all times and in rear seats where fitted.
- Random breath-testing takes place. Never drive under the influence of alcohol.
- Virtually all vehicles run on *sin plomo* (unleaded) or *gasoil* (diesel).
- Petrol stations are normally open 6am–10pm, although larger ones (which are often self-service) are open 24 hours. Virtually all accept credit cards.
- If you have a breakdown, follow the instructions given in the car rental documentation; most of the international and local rental firms provide a rescue service.

CAR RENTAL

The leading international car rental companies are represented at Ibiza airport and in the main towns and resorts. Many local companies, including Moto Luis (☎ 971 34 05 21; www.motoluis.com), offer competitive rates. A rental car is essential for reaching those out-of-the-way coves, but note that if you have an accident on a dirt road, many insurance policies are invalid.

Being there

TOURIST OFFICES

Ibiza

- 1 Passeig de Vara de Rey, Eivissa ☎ 971 30 19 00 ☻ May–Oct Mon–Fri 9–8, Sat 9–7, Sun 9–1; Nov–Apr Mon–Fri 9–7, Sat 9–6, Sun 9–3

- Marià Riquer Wallis s/n, Santa Eulària ☎ 971 33 07 28 ☻ May–Oct Mon–Fri 9:30–1:30, 5–7:30, Sat 9:30–2; Nov–Apr Mon–Fri 8:30–3, Sat 9–2

- Passeig de Ses Fonts s/n, Sant Antoni ☎ 971 31 40 05 ☻ May–Oct Mon–Fri 9–2, 4–9, Sat, Sun 9:30–1; Nov–Apr Mon–Sat 9–1

Formentera

- Port de La Savina, Formentera ☎ 971 32 20 57 ☻ Mon–Fri 10–8, Sat, Sun 10–3

MONEY

The euro (€) is the official currency of Spain. 100 cents = €1. Travellers' cheques and cash can be changed at most banks. Visa, Access and MasterCard are generally accepted in hotels and restaurants.

TIPS/GRATUITIES

Yes ✓ No ✗		
Restaurants (if service not included)	✓	10%
Cafés/bars (if service not included)	✓	change
Tour guides	✓	€2
Taxis	✓	10%
Chambermaids	✓	€1
Porters	✓	€1

INTERNET AND POSTAL SERVICES

Ibiza has plenty of internet cafés, with broadband, where you can surf, download and often burn digital pictures to CDs. Formentera is less well wired, but does have a few places. An hour online costs around €2.50.

Post offices (correos in Spanish, correus in Catalan) are generally open Mon–Fri 8:30–2:30, Sat 9:30–1, but some also open in the afternoon

Mon–Fri. The main post office in Eivissa is at 67 Avinguda d'Isidor Macabich (☎ 971 39 97 69 🕐 Mon–Fri 8:30–8:30, Sat 9:30–2), and on Formentera at 30 Pla del Rei, Sant Francesc (☎ 971 32 22 43 🕐 Mon–Fri 8:30–8:30, Sat 9:30–1).

TELEPHONES
Public telephones *(teléfonos)* take coins and phonecards, which are available from post offices *(correos)* and *tabacos*. You can't make reverse-charge calls from a call box. To call the operator dial 002.

Mobile-phone users note that overseas roaming charges can be steep. If your phone is not locked to a provider, consider using a local SIM card, which costs about €12, for the duration of your stay. Movistar is the most popular Spanish mobile network.

International dialling codes
From Ibiza and Formentera (Spain) to:
UK: 00 44

Ireland: 00 353
Germany: 00 49
USA: 00 1
Netherlands: 00 31

EMBASSIES AND CONSULATES
UK ☎ 971 30 18 18 (Eivissa)   USA ☎ 971 40 37 07 (Mallorca)
Ireland ☎ 971 72 25 04 (Mallorca)

HEALTH ADVICE
Sun advice The sunniest (and hottest) months are July and August, with an average of 10 hours of sun per day (➤ 22 for average temperatures). Particularly during these months you should avoid the midday sun and use a strong sunblock.

Drugs Prescription and non-prescription drugs and medicines are available from pharmacies *(farmácias)*, distinguished by a large green cross. Pharmacies are able to dispense many drugs which would be available only on prescription in other countries.

Safe water Tap water is very saline and undrinkable. Mineral water is cheap to buy and is sold as *con gaz* (carbonated) and *sin gaz* (still). Drink plenty of water during hot weather.

PLANNING

PERSONAL SAFETY

The national police force, the Policía Nacional
(brown uniforms) keep law and order in urban
areas. Some resorts have their own tourist-friendly
Policía Turística. If you need a police station ask for
la comisaría. To help prevent crime:

- Do not carry more cash than you need.
- Do not leave valuables on the beach or poolside.
- Beware of pickpockets in markets, tourist sights
  or crowded places.
- Avoid walking alone in dark alleys at night.

Police assistance: ☎ 112 from any call box

ELECTRICITY

The power supply in Ibiza and Formentera is 220–225 volts.

Sockets accept two-round-pin-style plugs, so an adaptor is needed for
most non-Continental appliances and a transformer for appliances
operating on 100–120 volts.

OPENING HOURS

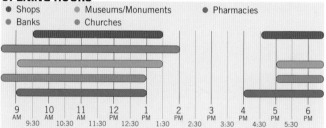

- Shops
- Banks
- Museums/Monuments
- Churches
- Pharmacies

In addition to the times shown above, large department stores, as well as
supermarkets and shops in tourist resorts, may open outside these times,
especially in summer. In general, pharmacies, banks and shops close on
Saturday afternoon, though banks stay open until 4:30pm Monday to
Thursday, October to May, but close Saturday, June to September.

The opening times of museums are just a rough guide; some are open
longer hours in summer, while hours are reduced in winter. Most
museums close on Mondays.

LANGUAGE

Eivissenc, the local dialect of Catalan, is the language you're most likely to hear in country areas, though Castilian Spanish is more common in towns and resorts. Catalan shares features with French and Spanish, but sounds nothing like either and is emphatically a language, not a dialect. Though Spanish will certainly get you by, it is polite to know some Catalan.

bank	*banc*	travellers' cheque	*xec de viatge*
exchange office	*oficina de canvi*	credit card	*carta de crèdit*
post office	*correus*	exchange rate	*tant per cent*
coin	*moneda*	commission charge	*comissió*
banknote	*bitllet de banc*	cashier	*caixer*
cheque	*xec*	change/currency	*camvi*
café/pub/bar	*cafè/celler/bar*	main course	*segón plat*
breakfast	*berenar*	dessert	*postres*
lunch/dinner	*dinar/sopar*	bill	*cuenta*
table	*taula*	beer/wine	*cervesa/vi*
waiter/waitress	*cambrer/cambrera*	water	*aigua*
starter	*primer plat*	coffee	*café*
aeroplane/airport	*avió/aeroport*	return ticket	*anar i tornar*
train/bus	*tren/autobús*	non-smoking	*no fumar*
station	*estació*	car/petrol	*cotxe/gasolina*
boat/port	*vaixell/port*	bus stop	*la parada*
ticket	*bitllet*	how do I get to...?	*per anar a...?*
single ticket	*senzill-a*	where is...?	*on és...?*
yes/no	*si/no*	you're welcome	*de res*
please	*per favor*	how are you?	*com va?*
thank you	*gràcies*	do you speak	*parla anglès?*
welcome	*de res*	English?	
hello/goodbye	*hola/adéu*	I don't understand	*no ho entenc*
good morning	*bon dia*	how much?	*quant es?*
good afternoon	*bona tarda*	open/closed	*obert/tancat*
goodnight	*bona nit*	today	*avui*
excuse me	*perdoni*	tomorrow	*demà*

Best places to see

1

Cala d'Hort

Tucked into a sheltered fold on Ibiza's southeastern coast, Cala d'Hort is one of the island's loveliest bays.

A *cala* is a small bay, of which there are scores dotted around the rugged coast of Ibiza. Cala d'Hort is very special indeed, with pellucid water, a gently shelving shingle-and-sandy beach and the dramatic islet of Es Vedrà – which rises abruptly to a height of 378m (1,240ft) – directly offshore.

This bay is exquisite, its 200m (220yd) beach framed by rocks and with a backdrop of steep cliffs and pine trees. If possible, try to stay until sunset: Cala d'Hort faces west and the sun dying into the Mediterranean horizon is another reason for the bay's popularity. The view from the cliff-top car park above the bay's southern end is magnificent.

Nothing this idyllic can be a secret, and the bay gets busy in the height of summer, though as there are no resorts close by it rarely gets too crowded. You'll find two good seafood restaurants here; the best views are from Es Boldado on the north side of the bay.

To reach Cala d'Hort, turn off the main road from Es Cubells to Sant Josep, or from Sant Josep to Cala Vedella.

🔁 2C 🖂 At the southwestern tip of the island
🍴 El Carmen (€), at the beach, or Es Boldado (€€; ➤ 58), reached by a short walk around the fishermen's huts or by a rough track from the Cala Vedella road

2 Catedral

The cathedral stands on one of the holiest sites of Ibiza: there was a Moorish mosque here and, prior to that, a Roman temple.

It is thought that the Romans chose the site because a Carthaginian temple (dedicated to the god Eshmum) occupied it, giving the site a history of worship going back 2,500 years. With the ousting of the Moors, a fine Gothic-style church, with a handsome Italian-style bell tower, was built. The church was largely completed by the mid-14th century, though substantial 18th-century modifications transformed the interior from

brooding Gothic to gaudy baroque that's verging on the kitsch. It was granted cathedral status in 1782.

The whitewashed interior contains a few interesting works of art, but the better pieces have been removed to the cathedral museum on the south side of the nave. One of the best exhibits here is a silver monstrance plate (the 'dish' used to hold the Host at Roman Catholic Masses) made in Mallorca in the 15th century. Look, too, for the altarpiece of Sant Macià by a 15th-century Tarragonian master, and some Renaissance-era choir books.

One interesting feature of the cathedral is its dedication, which is to the island's patron saint. No surprise there, but in this warmest of European islands the patron saint is Santa Maria de las Neus, the Virgin of the Snows. The reason is that in the calendar of Spanish holy days that of the Virgin of the Snows fell closest to when the Christians captured the island from the Moors.

✠ *Eivissa 3d* ✉ Plaça de la Catedral, Dalt Vila
🕐 Cathedral and museum daily 9:30–1:30, 5–8
💷 Cathedral free; museum inexpensive 🍽 La Ventana
(€€), Sa Carrossa, Dalt Vila 🚌 Bus 45 from Vara de Rey
❓ A sign on the cathedral door notes 'When you don't have the right clothes, don't come in', ie no swimming costumes

3 Dalt Vila

Dominating any view of Eivissa, Ibiza's capital, is Dalt Vila, a marvellous medieval town still encircled by its old walls.

The walls of Dalt Vila ('high town') are one of Europe's finest examples of medieval military architecture, and have been declared a UNESCO World Heritage Monument. Within them, and in the narrow streets of the town below, you will experience a sense of the history of Ibiza.

The walls date from the 16th century, when Carlos (Charles) V decided to reinforce the island's defences against Turkish pirates and the threat they represented of a new Saracen invasion. Charles called in Juan Calvi, the Italian military engineer who had already completed new defences at Mallorca and Barcelona. But though Calvi was responsible for the original design, legend has it that his local foreman, a man known only as El Fratin, changed the plan frequently, expanding the defences and creating most of what we see today. Around the walls there are seven *baluards* (bastions) on which artillery was mounted.

Within the walls are some of Ibiza's most atmospheric streets. Those in the upper town near the castle and cathedral are lined with the former mansions of the aristocracy, while those

closer to the port are more humble. Bustling Plaça de la Vila and nearby Sa Carrossa are thick with elegant restaurants and cafés.

Dalt Vila also boasts the best of Ibiza's museums (➤ 78–79). The Museu Puget has the paintings of one of Ibiza's most renowned artists, while the Museu Arqueològic and the Centre d'Interpretació Madina Yabisa provide historical perspectives.

✚ *Eivissa 2d* ✉ The old town of Eivissa 👋 Free 🍴 Plaza del Sol (€€), in the Plaça del Sol close to the Baluard des Portal Nou 🚌 Bus 45 from Vara de Rey

4 La Mola, Formentera

For rugged grandeur, there is nothing that compares with the elevated plateau that forms Formentera's Cap de la Mola, which has a wild, desolate beauty all of its own.

From Sant Francesc, Formentera's 'capital', three roads head off for the island's coasts. One reaches La Savina, the port for Ibiza, another heads for Cap de Barbària, and the third for the eastern headland

of La Mola. The latter ends at the La Mola lighthouse, built to warn seafarers of the dangerous rocks that lie below it. The rock of the high plateau of Formentera's eastern tip is exposed here, the limestone forming a pavement of huge flat slabs. Windblown soil has gathered in the gaps between the slabs and hardy plants have rooted.

Jules Verne was so inspired by the isolation of the place that he used the Mola lighthouse as inspiration for his novel *Journey Around the Solar System*. The view from the headland is magnificent, the rocks themselves – in shades of red and grey – being particularly picturesque against the turquoise sea. It feels like the end of the world.

The lighthouse at La Mola was built in 1861 by Emilio Pou. First lit by vegetable oil, it had a range of about 55km (34 miles). The fuel was changed from oil to paraffin and then to petrol and finally to electricity when Formentera was electrified in the 1960s. Interestingly, the upgrading of the light to modern power has meant only a modest increase in range, to 65km (40 miles). Unfortunately, the lighthouse can only be seen from the outside as it is not open to the public.

🟥 *Formentera 8b* 📧 The extreme eastern end of Formentera 🍴 Codice Luna (€), at the end of the road, near the lighthouse 🚌 Es Pujols–Sant Ferran–La Mola

5 Nuestra Señora de Jesús

In Jesús, a former hamlet now the size of a couple of kilometres north of Eivissa, is one of Ibiza's most charming churches, just to the east of the centre.

The church of Nuestra Señora de Jesús, usually referred to as Jesús, is a magnificent building, beautifully arcaded on one side and with the typically austere Romanesque-style frontage popular in 15th-century Spain. The solidity of the construction owes much to its history, such village churches having been built by the villagers themselves rather than by craft builders, each man lending his own particular skills and style. The church also often served as a refuge during pirate attacks.

It is not, however, for the exterior that the church is famous. Inside is the island's greatest work of art, the retable, or altar screen. This triptych (a three-panelled painting) is thought to have been completed early in the 16th century by the Valencian artist Rodrigo de Osona. The base of the retable shows the seven key events in the life of the Virgin, from the Annunciation to the Assumption. Above is the Virgin and Child, a work of intimacy and gentleness, quite different in character from the more formal poses that are normally seen in paintings of the period. Above is St Francis of

Assisi receiving the stigmata. Above again is Christ appearing to St Gregory. The side panels of the triptych show further scenes from the lives of the saints.

The church is normally locked, but you can usually get the key from the nearby bar, Bon Lloc, or you can see the retable before or after services.

✚ 9D ✉ Just off the Eivissa–Cala Llonga road 🖐 Free 🍴 Bon Lloc (€€), just west of the church 🚌 Bus 15, which connects Eivissa and Cala Llonga

6 Platja de ses Illetes, Formentera

Formentera is blessed with some of the Mediterranean's best beaches, wonderful expanses of soft pale sand lapped by transparent water, but Platja de ses Illetes has to be the cream of the crop.

Here nature is reduced to its basic elements – the clarity of the sea and the whiteness of the sand – and it's hard not to be overwhelmed by the sheer beauty of the scene. It's no surprise that a small fleet of super-yachts is usually anchored in the bay.

Illetes forms the western half of a slim finger of land, the Trucadors peninsula, which pokes north from La Savina. The eastern half of this peninsula

forms another beach, known as Tango or Llevant, so you can choose either an east- or a west-facing stretch of sand, as one is only a few steps from the other. There are a couple of stylish *chiringuitos* behind the beach, including the hip Juan y Andrea. At the southern end is the Molí des Carregador, a windmill that's now a top-quality seafood restaurant (Es Molí de Sal, ➤ 152). Or try Pirates, at the north end, for a less extravagant meal.

From the northern tip of Illetes, if conditions are calm, it's possible to wade (or even swim) to the island of S'Espalmador (➤ 141).

🕂 *Formentera 3e* ✉ 5km (3 miles) north of La Savina 🚌 La Savina–Illetes–Es Pujols ❓ Cars are charged €4 and scooters €2 to access the peninsula in summer

7 Platja de ses Salines

Of Ibiza's fifty or so beaches, Platja de ses Salines (Salines beach) attracts one of the most stylish crowds.

In the height of summer, sun loungers are occupied by people in the fashion and music industries, and in the beachside restaurants you may spot the occasional celeb or Spanish footballer enjoying a lobster lunch.

It's not difficult to understand Salines' appeal. There's none of the ugly resort sprawl that taints many Ibizan bays, as the beach is fringed by a backdrop of pine trees and sand dunes, and the only concession to commerce, apart from several *chiringuitos*, are beach hawkers selling CDs, sunglasses and sarongs.

As you head south down the beach, the denizens of Salines sport less and less in the way of swimwear, and the tiny final bays are often manned

by naked sun-worshippers.

If you continue beyond the last of these bays you pass over a rocky shelf before emerging at a lonely lighthouse, the southernmost point on the island, which gazes out over a string of rocky islets to Formentera.

Visit Salines beach outside the main tourist season and it's a very different scene, when the sands are likely to be all yours.

🚌 6B 📧 11km (7 miles) south of Eivissa 🚏 Regular bus service from Eivissa in the summer (bus 11)

8 Santa Eulària des Riu

Ibiza's third-largest town is rare in that it has been extended for the benefit of the tourist industry without losing its charm.

Santa Eulària des Riu (or Santa Eulalia del Rio) is the only town in the Balearics to be set on a river, though it must be said that the river is barely more than a stream and in summer often dries to little more than a trickle between pools. Both river and town are named after the saint to whom the church on nearby Puig de Missa (➤ 110–111) is dedicated.

Santa Eulària grew up as a market town for the local area, although the old quarter has vanished beneath a strict grid of modern streets as the town continues to expand. But Santa Eulària was also one of the first places in Ibiza to attract foreign visitors, particularly British actors, and in its heyday

in the 1960s and 1970s Laurence Olivier and Elizabeth Taylor stayed here, while Denholm Elliott and Terry-Thomas set up home nearby. There's a modern seafront and marina, but the development of these areas has been fairly thoughtful, particularly the marina, which has plenty of excellent restaurants, boutiques and, of course, bobbing boats galore.

The other main area worth exploring is the historic hilltop of Puig de Missa, just east of the centre, crowned by a mighty church with a

semicircular defence tower, and also boasting the Museu Etnològic d'Eivissa i Formentera, a museum dedicated to the islands' rural traditions.

➕ 21H ✉ On Ibiza's eastern coast, 14km (9 miles) northeast of Eivissa 🍽 Several choices in Carrer de Sant Vicent (➤ 133) 🚌 Santa Eulària is served by buses from all parts of the island

9 Santa Gertrudis

Smack in the centre of the island, with good road connections to all corners of Ibiza, is Santa Gertrudis, a delightful, easy-going Ibizan village famous for its artists.

Its glory days as an agricultural centre may be long gone, and rather haphazard development has detracted from its sleepy image, but it retains village charm at its core, where visitors and foreign residents gather to enjoy the many cafés and restaurants. The choice includes La Plaza (€€), with

exquisite French cooking in a rustic Spanish setting, and a modern deli-café called Musset (€€), but perhaps the most enjoyable venue remains the long-running Bar Costa (➤ 133) – an unpretentious locals' local where legs of *jamon serrano* hang from the ceiling and the walls are filled with paintings given by artists in lieu of payment.

A visit to Santa Gertrudis is about soaking up the scene and people-watching, but worth seeing also is the village church, a handsome whitewashed structure with a broad facade and a tiny belfry. The village also has Ibiza's only auction house, Casi Todo (www.casitodo.com), where everything from classic cars and vintage cameras to second-hand tools goes under the hammer each fortnight.

✚ 17H ⊠ 13km (8 miles) north of Eivissa 🚌 22, 25 from Eivissa, 28 from Santa Eulària

10 Ses Salines, Formentera

Whereas parts of the Ibizan *salines*, pools for the extraction of salt, are still worked, those on Formentera are no longer used for salt production and today form a nature reserve.

The islands' *salines* have been prized for centuries, the salt being used to preserve food on long sea voyages.

The salt pans and the neighbouring lagoons of Estany des Peix and Estany Pudent are rich in wildlife. The curious mix of sandy shoreline and dunes and the expanses of high-salinity water supports a varied collection of plant life and a number of exotic birds, including flamingos, which often refuel and rest here in late summer. The lakes

are also strangely beautiful, with patches of pinkish water and a fringe of old salt heaps.

Estany Pudent (the name means 'smelly lagoon' – very appropriate when low water levels expose weeds that quickly rot in the burning sun) is the best place for birdwatchers; over 250 species of birds having been recorded. Several use the lagoon as a stopover, but there are resident colonies of egrets, stints, herons and other waders.

✚ *Formentera 3d* ✉ The *salines* and Estany Pudent are on the north side of the La Savina–Sant Francesc road, while the Estany des Peix is on the south side of the highway 🍴 El Tiburón (€€; ➤ 59) 🚌 Es Pujols–Sant Francesc–La Savina

Best things to do

Great places to have lunch

El Bigotes (€€)

This humble little fish restaurant is right by the waves and you lunch on fish caught and cooked by the owner or members of his family. You have to book in person at least a day in advance.

✉ Cala Mastella ☎ 971 39 33 60 🕒 Easter–Nov daily 12–6

Es Boldado (€€)

Specializes in seafood, paella and lobster, with amazing views of Es Vedrà from its lofty terrace.

✉ Cala d'Hort ☎ 626 49 45 37 🕒 Daily 1pm–midnight

Can Rafalet (€€)

With tables on the terrace next to the Med, Can Rafalet offers wonderful views and fine seafood.

✉ Es Caló, Formentera ☎ 971 32 70 77 🕒 May–Sep daily 1–4, 8–12

El Chiringuito (€€)

A relaxed place, on a tiny cove just north of Sant Antoni.

✉ Cala Gracioneta ☎ 971 34 83 38 🕐 May–Oct daily 10am–1am

Eden, Hacienda Na Xamena (€€€)

The most expensive buffet lunch on Ibiza, but what a location, high on the coastal cliffs of northern Ibiza.

✉ 3km (2 miles) west of Port de Sant Miquel ☎ 971 33 45 00 🕐 Daily 1–4, 8–11

La Paloma (€€)

Idyllic family-run restaurant famed for its bohemian countryside atmosphere and its fabulously fresh Italian cuisine.

✉ Sant Llorenç ☎ 971 32 55 43 🕐 Daily 1–4, 8–12 (closed Sun mid-Oct to Jun)

Plaza del Sol (€€)

Close to one of Dalt Vila's *baluards* (bastions), shaded by spreading trees and with a classic view of the harbour.

✉ Plaça del Sol, Dalt Vila ☎ 971 39 07 73 🕐 Easter–Sep daily 1–3, 8:30–1

Sa Caleta (€€)

A marvellously relaxed, family-run *chiringuito*, with excellent fish and rice dishes. It's popular for a lazy Sunday lunch.

✉ Sa Caleta ☎ 971 18 70 95 🕐 Daily 1pm–1am

Sa Punta (€€€)

Chic, well-regarded restaurant in a great beachside setting.

✉ Talamanca (northern end) ☎ 971 34 56 72 🕐 Apr–Oct daily 11am–3am

El Tiburón (€€)

Effortlessly classy and with tables virtually on the sand and shaded by coastal pines, this *chiringuito* is one of Formentera's best.

✉ Platja Cavall d'en Borràs, 1km (0.6 miles) northeast of La Savina, Formentera ☎ 659 63 89 45 🕐 May–Sep daily 10–7

Great clubs

Amnèsia

This legendary venue put Ibiza on the map in the 1980s when DJ
Alfredo mixed house with British indie, a slice of reggae and
random eclectica to create the Balearic Beat. Today it's a temple of
trance and hard house, and is host to British superclubs like
Cream, as well as the island's only foam party.

✉ On the Sant Antoni–Eivissa road, at the 5km post ☎ 971 19 80 41;
www.amnesia.es 🕓 Jun–Sep midnight–6am

Eden

This is Sant Antoni's pre-eminent club, with a capacity of around
3,000 and a roster of big-name British DJs.

✉ Carrer Salvador Espiriu (just off the harbourfront), Sant Antoni
☎ 971 80 32 40; www.edenibiza.com 🕓 Jun–Sep

Pacha

The original, and still the classiest, club in Ibiza, though the VIP section is starting to take over the main room. DJs like Frankie Knuckles, David Morales and Erick Morillo set up residences here in the summer, although with a myriad rooms, it's possible to find your own niche, be it salsa, vocal house, R 'n' B or funk. Pacha is the only Ibizan club to open all year round.

✉ Avenida del 8 d'Agost, Eivissa ☎ 971 31 36 12; www.pacha.es
🕐 8pm–6am (winter: weekends only)

Privilege

The largest club in the world, holding 10,000 people, Privilege hosts some epic events, but the huge space can be echoingly empty on quiet nights. The venue is simply colossal, with a vast main room (complete with swimming pool), the infamous Coco Loco bar, a chillout dome and a garden zone.

✉ Sant Rafel ☎ 971 19 81 60; www.privilegeibiza.com 🕐 Jun–late Sep

Space

Now totally transformed, this is the island's most modern venue, with multiple rooms and an army of DJs in high season. Sunday sessions are an Ibizan institution. There are two dance terraces, a chillout terrace and the main club arena (with a Who's Who of club culture manning the decks).

✉ Platja d'en Bossa ☎ 971 39 67 94; www.space-ibiza.es
🕐 Jun–late Sep

Xueño

This small, classy, Italian club, with an intimate feel and a stylish chillout terrace, has put Formentera on the clubbing map. DJs and artists including Claudio Coccoluto, Robert Owens and Pacha's DJ Pippi have performed here.

✉ Es Pujols, on Sant Ferrán road ☎ 971 32 91 60; www.xueno.com
🕐 Jun–Aug

Best beaches

IBIZA

Aigües Blanques An exposed, slimline nudist beach that's not been developed for tourism. Limited facilities.

Cala Bassa Backed by pine trees, this broad beach attracts many visitors from Sant Antoni. Excellent facilities (► 108).

Cala Benirràs Northern Ibiza's finest beach is in a gorgeous inlet with safe swimming. Excellent facilities (► 96).

Cala Compte There are several small coves here, and the water is crystal clear. Some facilities.

Cala d'Hort (► 36–37).

Cala Jondal Pebble beach with great restaurants. Its beach clubs have made it one of the island's hotspots. Good facilities (► 114).

Cala Mastella A marvellous little cove with excellent swimming, but limited facilities (► 98).

Cala Salada About 4km (2.5 miles) north of Sant Antoni, this little bay has a good restaurant and sheltered waters. Limited facilities (► 98–99).

Cala Vedella A small beach in a cove popular with yachties. Excellent facilities include a dive school (► 99).

Cala Xarraca Small, with limited facilities, but very beautiful. The local mud is said to have healing properties (► 100).

Figueretes On the south side of Eivissa, this built-up bay is within walking distance of the capital. Good facilities.

Platja d'en Bossa A continuation of Figueretes. It's a package-holiday resort, also known for its beach clubs, so tends to get crowded, but it's not difficult to find a quiet spot at the far southern end. Excellent facilities.

Platja des Cavallet A nudist beach with fine sands and great restaurants. It's popular with gay men. Excellent facilities.

Platja des Codolar Expansive pebble beach, just south of the airport runway, but rarely gets busy. Limited facilities.

Platja de ses Salines Sand dunes and salt pans divide Platja des Cavallet from this chic beach (► 48). Excellent facilities.

Talamanca Just north of Eivissa, Talamanca is an attractive, crescent-shaped sandy beach with excellent facilities (► 126).

FORMENTERA
Cala Saona The island's only cove beach. Good facilities (► 139).

Llevant A gorgeous stretch of sand on the eastern side of the Trucadors peninsula (► 46–47). Facilities are reasonable, but decreasing as you move towards S'Espalmador.

Platja de ses Illetes (► 46–47).

Platja de Migjorn A huge, very beautiful beach, with clean white sand and equally clean blue water. Excellent facilities (► 146–147).

NB: 'Facilities' means the availability of food and drink, and the hire of water-sports equipment and sunbeds.

a walk around Punta de ses Portes

This walk begins on Ibiza's official nudist beach, so be prepared for strange looks as you pass by, particularly if you are carrying a camera with a long lens!

From the car park at Es Cavallet walk south along the beach, heading for the watchtower at the far end.

Walking on the beach is difficult, but the going can be made a little easier by keeping to the firmer sand which is near the water's edge. Alternatively, you could cross the sand dunes at the back of the beach to reach an easier track. The southern end of the beach is predominantly gay, as is the excellent Chiringay café/bar.

Whichever route you choose to follow, you will eventually reach the watchtower at Punta de ses Portes, which gazes southwards to the slab-like outline of low-lying Formentera on the horizon.

The first tower was built in the late 16th century, part of a network that ringed the coastline, to protect Ibiza against pirate attacks, but was abandoned in the 19th century. The name of the headland means the 'Cape of the Gates', the three offshore islets creating passages or 'gates' between Ibiza and Formentera. One is known as Illa des Penjats (Island of the Hanged) and was once the last stop for Ibizan criminals.

Returning by the western flank of the promontory, it's a 15-minute walk over a rocky shoreline to Sa Trinxa, the first of the chiringuitos on Salines beach.

This is where the beautiful people come to relax, and enjoy the eclectic music tastes of resident DJ Jonathan Grey.

From Sa Trinxa, it's a 20-minute hike along the sandy shoreline to the northern end of the beach, from where you can head inland through the glistening salines to the car park at Es Cavallet.

Distance 9km (5.5 miles)
Time 3 hours
Start/end point The car park at Es Cavallet beach (Platja des Cavallet) ➕ 8A
Lunch La Escollera (€€€; ➤ 132) ✉ Es Cavallet beach

Best activities

CYCLING AND MOUNTAIN BIKING

Ibiza and Formentera have 'green routes' that can be explored on mountain bikes. In Ibiza a map is available from the tourist office giving details of routes – the best are in the rural north and northwest – or go to the sports section of www.ibiza.travel.

In Formentera a pamphlet includes details of 19 cycle/mountain bike itineraries, together with a further nine walking routes.

All of the islands' cycle-hire shops stock mountain bikes as well as road cycles, and most also provide crash helmets with bike hire.

Kadani ✉ On the road to Es Canar, in Santa Eulària ☎ 971 33 92 64; www.ibiza-activa.com

DIVING

Ibiza and Formentera have some of the clearest waters in the Mediterranean, with visibility up to 40m (130ft). With summer water temperatures rising to 26°C (80°F), this makes the islands an ideal place to dive. All divers have access to the decompression chamber at the La Sirena club in Sant Antoni.

Ibiza Diving ✉ Port Desportiu, Santa Eulària ☎ 971 33 29 49; www.ibiza-diving.com

Sant Miquel ✉ Port de Sant Miquel ☎ 971 33 45 39; www.divingcenter-sanmiguel.com

Sea Horse Club ✉ Port des Torrent ☎ 971 34 64 38; www.seahorsedivingibiza.com

Subfari ✉ Cala Portinatx ☎ 971 33 31 83

HORSE RIDING

Ibiza seems to have been made for exploration on horseback, and specific tracks have been created to explore the wilder parts of the island. There are several schools and organizations offering lessons and hacks, the following offers options for people of all ages looking for a gentle way of exploring the island's stunning scenery.

Can Mayans ✉ Santa Gertrudis ☎ 971 18 73 88

KAYAKING AND SAILING

At beaches such as Cala Bassa, Cala Vedella or Cala Benirràs you can hire pedalos or sit-on kayaks, while at larger resorts such as Platja d'en Bossa and Cala Tarida you can hire windsurf boards and sailing dinghies. The following offer sailing and kayaking lessons:

Anfibios ✉ Platja d'en Bossa ☎ 971 30 39 15

CC Cats ✉ South end of Ses Salines beach ☎ 908 63 06 32

Club Nàutico ✉ Sant Antoni de Portmany ☎ 971 34 06 45

Vela Náutica ✉ Sant Antoni de Portmany ☎ 908 53 90 31

WALKING

The islands are ideal for walking. Much of the coast of Ibiza is followed by the Ruta de Falcó. In addition to this long-distance trail, major towns on Ibiza and Formentera produce leaflets on local walks. One idea is a 23km (14-mile) route exploring the uplands north of Sant Antoni, linking with Santa Agnès de Corona. Or you can climb Sa Talaia (➤ 121), Ibiza's highest peak. The website www.ecoibiza.com offers a number of 'secret' walks.

WATER PARKS

There are two excellent water parks on Ibiza:

Aguamar ✉ Platja d'en Bossa ☎ 971 39 67 90 🕐 May–Oct daily 10–7 🚌 Eivissa–Platja d'en Bossa

Aqualandia ✉ Cap Martinet, Talamanca ☎ 971 19 24 11 🕐 Jun–Sep daily 10–7 🚌 Eivissa–Cap Martinet

Markets

IBIZA
Club Punta Arabí

The original 'hippy market', though much of the jewellery and clothes are mass-produced imports rather than items made on the island.

✉ Es Canar ⏰ Wed 9–7

Las Dalias

Arts, crafts and clothes, some interesting and original.

✉ At the 12km post on the main road near Sant Carles ☎ 971 33 50 42
⏰ Sat 9–7

La Marina

Mainly jewellery and souvenirs.

✉ Along the harbourfront, eastern end of Passeig des Moll, Eivissa
⏰ Every night Jun–Sep

Sant Antoni

Souvenirs, clothes, CDs, DVDs and jewellery.

✉ Around Plaça de l'Església, Sant Antoni ⏰ Every night Jun–Sep

Sant Jordi

Located in the hippodrome, which is a bit of a dust bowl. More of a car boot sale than a market, but always throws up some interesting stuff.

✉ Sant Jordi, 4km (2.5 miles) south of Eivissa Town ⏰ Sat 9–2

FORMENTERA
El Pilar de la Mola

A good-quality arts and crafts market.

✉ La Mola ⏰ May–Oct Wed and Sun 4–9pm

Stunning views

Ibiza

Gaze out to Es Vedrà from the Mirador del Savinar (➤ 104–105).

Enjoy sweeping views from Sa Talaia, the island's highest point (➤ 121, Sant Josep).

There's no finer view in Eivissa than from the summit of Dalt Vila (➤ 40–41).

Catch glimpses of rustic Ibiza as you travel along the Santa Agnès–Sant Mateu road.

The plunging sea cliffs of the northwest coast look their dizzying best from the open-air bar of the Hacienda hotel (➤ 130).

To capture Ibiza's glamour and hedonism in a single snapshot, head to the bars of La Marina, Eivissa, around midnight (➤ 78).

Settle in with a sundowner and enjoy the sunset at Sant Antoni's Sunset Strip (➤ 117).

Take a walk around the saltpans of Ses Salines, then head to the beautiful beach (➤ 126).

Formentera
Watch the huge red sun sizzle out of a vast empty seascape from La Mola (➤ 42–43).

Witness the improbably turquoise waters of Ses Illetes (➤ 46–47).

Exploring

With a beguiling climate, scores of idyllic cove beaches and glorious countryside, much of Ibiza and Formentera's natural beauty begs to be explored. Away from the resorts, it's easy to access pristine coastline and historic sites that date from Carthaginian times.

Both islands have strong counter-cultural traditions rooted in the 1960s, when hippies and beatniks first discovered them. This spirit endures in the arts, crafts and, arguably, clubbing scene. Few places in Europe have a population that is as tolerant or environmentally aware, and naturists and naturalists, fashionistas and families find the islands' appeal equally strong.

Above all, Ibiza is renowned for its nightlife, and the sheer spectacle is something to behold, as the clubs host legendary DJs night after night in summer. But it's also possible to avoid this scene if you want to, as there's room for everyone.

Eivissa (Ibiza Town)

There are few more dramatic sights on the Mediterranean coast than that of Eivissa's Old Town, Dalt Vila, especially when viewed from the sea, its walls and bastions rising above the rugged coast and turquoise water.

Under Franco's centralist regime only Castilian names were allowed in areas of Spain that had their own language or dialect. But today the island's capital has reverted to its Catalan name, Eivissa, echoing the ancient identities of the island – the Carthaginian *Ibosim*, the Greek *Ebysos*, the Roman *Ebusus* and the Moorish *Yebisah*.

Eivissa is a marvellous place in summer, low-key by day, high-octane by night, an exciting assault on the senses. Within its close confines it captures the essence of the island – Dalt Vila, Sa Penya, La Marina and the local coast offering quite different aspects of Ibiza. Go to Dalt Vila for historical Ibiza, to Sa Penya's tight-knit streets for boutiques and bars, to La Marina or the harbour for sea views and an array of restaurants and bars, or the nearby beaches for sun, sea and sand.

BALUARD DE SANT BERNAT

Between the cathedral (➤ 38–39) and the castle (➤ opposite) a narrow alley leads to the Baluard de Sant Bernat, from where there is a magnificent view of the south of the island, sweeping along the beaches of Figueretes and Platja d'en Bossa out to the island's tip near Ses Salines. Straight ahead is Formentera, while below is the scrubland of Es Soto, from where Catalan invaders are said to have launched their attack on the Moors in 1235.

✚ *Eivissa 3e* 💧 Free access

BALUARD DE SANTA LLÚCIA

Those following the line of the old walls – the circuit is a little under 2km (1.2 miles) and worth the effort – will eventually reach the triangular bastion of Baluard de Santa Llúcia, its long sides aligned with the harbour and the coast to give maximum range to its artillery. From the bastion there is a splendid view over the huddle of houses and narrow alleys of Sa Penya (➤ 86) to La Marina (➤ 78) and Eivissa's harbour.

✚ Eivissa 3d 🍴 La Torreta, Plaça de la Vila, near the Portal de ses Taules (€€; ➤ 92) 🖐 Free access

CASTELL

The Castell (Castle) stands across from the cathedral (➤ 38–39) and Archaeological Museum (➤ 79), though it's currently inaccessible and being converted into a Parador hotel (due to open around 2014). The castle dates from at least the time of the Moors and is almost certainly older. The numerous attempts at reconstruction, necessary both to modify the defences in line with changes in weaponry and to satisfy the desires of the latest island ruler, created an odd assortment of bits and pieces which required continuous upkeep. When the need for a fortress declined in the 19th century, maintenance stopped and the castle fell into disrepair.

✚ Eivissa 2d ✉ Plaça de la Catedral, Dalt Vila 🕐 Closed for restoration 🍴 The Plaza del Sol (€€), in the Plaça del Sol close to the Baluard des Portal Nou

CATEDRAL

Best places to see, pages 38–39.

CENTRE D'INTERPRETACIÓ MADINA YABISA

The Centre d'Interpretació Madina Yabisa, just off Plaça de la Catedral, takes up the historical narrative from the Museu Arqueològic (➤ 79). The latest addition to Eivissa's museum roster, its multimedia displays document the development of Eivissa as the Moorish port city Madina Yabisa from the 11th to 13th centuries. Part of the Islamic wall and two towers have been restored within the building.

✚ *Eivissa 2d* ✉ 2 Carrer Major, Dalt Vila ☎ 971 39 23 90 ◷ Apr to mid-Oct Tue–Sat 10–2, 5–8 (Jul, Aug 6–9), Sun 10–2; mid-Oct to Mar Tue–Sat 10–3, Sun 10–1 ✋ Moderate

DALT VILA

Best places to see, pages 40–41.

LA MARINA

This harbourside quarter is chic and happening, with a plethora of upmarket boutiques, plenty of restaurants and a smattering of decent bars. But great though La Marina is for shopping and dining, it is even better for people-watching. In recent years the area has

become the focus of the city's bar scene, and the club parades around midnight provide a taste of Ibiza's famous hedonism.

La Marina is very compact – from the seafront cafés to the walls of Dalt Vila or the market square is less than 200m (220yds) – so all of it can be examined in detail in a couple of hours. If you are really pressed for time head for the four short, parallel streets of Rimbau, Bisbe Torres, Azaria and Arubal to find the best shopping the area has to offer.

✚ *Eivissa 2c* 🍴 For lunch El Faro (€€; ➤ 91), on the harbourfront; for a budget dinner El Pirata (€) or Pasajeros (€; both ➤ 92)

MUSEU ARQUEOLÒGIC

The Archaeological Museum is an excellent museum of the history of Ibiza and Formentera. It is compact – though it does have a lot of steps – so a visit need only take an hour or so, but it will be a worthwhile hour, giving a useful insight into the lives of the Carthaginian, Roman and Moorish occupants of the islands. The Carthaginian remains are particularly good: look for images of the gods Baal (the destroyer) and Tanit (a fertility goddess). The displays have explanations in English as well as Spanish and Catalan.

✚ *Eivissa 3d* ✉ 3 Plaça de la Catedral, Dalt Vila ☎ 971 30 12 31
🕐 Apr–Sep Tue–Sat 10–2, 6–8, Sun 10–2; Oct–Mar Tue–Sun 9–3
✋ Moderate 🍴 The Plaza del Sol (€€; ➤ 92), in the Plaça del Sol

MUSEU PUGET

The Museu Puget, a little farther down Carrer Major than the Centre d'Interpretació Madina Yabisa, completes the Dalt Vila museums, displaying paintings and sketches by Ibizan-born artists Narcís Puget Viñas and his son Narcís Puget Riquer. It's worth a visit as much for the impressive foyer of its Renaissance mansion as for the exhibits.

✚ *Eivissa 2d* ✉ 18 Carrer Major, Dalt Vila ☎ 971 39 21 47 🕐 May–Sep Tue–Fri 10–1:30, 5–8, Sat, Sun 10–1:30; Oct–Apr Tue–Fri 10–1:30, 5–6, Sat, Sun 10–1:30 ✋ Free

a walk around Eivissa

This walk starts by the sea.

Cross into Plaça d'Antoni Riguer and bear right to Plaça de Sa Tertiúlia. Turn sharp left (look for the San Telmo restaurant sign).

At the T-junction turn left, then first right, to pass the Mercat Vell (Old Market) in Plaça de la Constitució.

Go up the ramp through Portal de ses Taules (▶ 84) to Plaça de la Vila. Turn sharp left to the edge of Sa Carrossa, then left again. The Museum of Contemporary Art (currently closed) is ahead: turn right along the old wall.

The seated figure in Sa Carrossa is Isidor Macabich, a writer and historian of Ibiza and Formentera.

Follow the wall to Baluard de Santa Llúcia (▶ 77). Turn right towards Sant Domènec (▶ 88). Go up steps into Plaça d'Espanya. Bear right through the square and go straight along Carrer de Pere Tur. Turn left up steps and continue past the El Corsario Hotel. Go sharp left up steps to reach a T-junction. Turn right, going under an arch, to reach a T-junction. Turn left, and pass the Centre d'Interpretació Madina Yabisa (▶ 78) to reach Plaça de la Catedral.

Here are the cathedral itself (➤ 38–39), the Archaeological Museum (➤ 79) and the Castle (➤ 77).

Return down Carrer Major, past the Museu Puget (➤ 79), bearing right along Carrer de Sant Ciriac, then right again. Go left down steps beside the Seminari.

The old seminary has been converted into apartments.

From here steps lead down to Carrer Sant Josep, and then down again and to the right towards Plaça del Sol. Return back via narrow Carrer Santa Creu to Plaça de la Vila, and reverse the outward route back to the harbour.

Distance 2km (1.2 miles)
Time 2–3 hours, depending on the museums visited
Start/end point Corsairs Monument, near the harbour ✚ *Eivissa 3c*
Lunch Plaza del Sol (€€; ➤ 92) ✉ Plaça del Sol, close to the Baluard des Portal Nou ☎ 971 39 07 73

PASSEIG DE VARA DE REY

Close to La Marina is the heart of colonial late 19th-century Eivissa. Head for the Passeig de Vara de Rey, in the centre of which stands a monument to one of Ibiza's most famous sons: Joachím Vara de Rey, an army general who died during the Spanish-American war over Cuba in 1889. This elegant boulevard is lined with cafés and upmarket clothing stores, as well as Eivissa's best bookshop, Llibreria Vara de Rey, which also sells foreign newspapers.

✚ *Eivissa 1c* 🍴 Alfredo's (➤ 91)

PLAÇA D'ESPANYA

At the extreme eastern edge of Dalt Vila lies Plaça d'Espanya, another of the famous landmarks of the old town. Within there is a reclining statue of Guillem de Montgri, one of the noblemen who captured the island in 1235.

The Ajuntament (Town Hall), which opens onto the square, occupies part of a large white building erected in the 17th century as a monastery for Dominican priests. Of the monastery, only the church (Sant Domènec, ➤ 88) remains.

From Plaça d'Espanya two excellent old streets head off westwards. Carrer de Pere Tur has several fine mansions, one of which, Casa Riquer, was built by Antoni Riquer, among Ibiza's most famous – and, from the fine style of the house, most successful – pirates. Carrer Major has an array of equally fine houses.

✚ *Eivissa 3d* 🍴 Alfredo's (€€; ➤ 91) or Bon Profit (€; ➤ 91)

PLAÇA DES PARC

Eivissa's most enjoyable place for a coffee or a beer is Plaça des Parc, just north of Passeig de Vara de Rey. This small square is pedestrianized, so children can run about freely, and the imposing walls of Dalt Vila rise above it, so the setting is impressive. Most of the dozen or so café-restaurants are casual and inexpensive, and bar prices are well below those of the port. You'll find a small supermarket in the eastern corner of the square, and plenty of boutiques in the nearby streets.

✚ *Eivissa 2c* 🍴 Many, including Bon Profit (€; ➤ 91)

PORTAL DE SES TAULES

Close to the market square (Plaça de la Constitució) of Sa Penya, the oldest section of the town outside the old walls, is the most imposing of the gates into the old town. The inscription above the gate notes that Felipe (Philip) II was responsible for its construction in 1585. The portal is decorated with the king's coat-of-arms and a pair of Roman statues unearthed during construction work. The inscription on one of them suggests it was originally raised to the goddess Juno.

Passing through the gateway (note the thickness of the wall: Charles V ordered that it should be 2m/6ft thick) you will reach the Pati d'Armes, the arsenal square. This beautifully colonnaded square has been restored, as has the archway that connects it to the equally delightful Plaça de la Vila.

✚ *Eivissa 3d* 🍴 Several choices nearby in Plaça de la Vila, including La Torreta (€€; ➤ 92)

PUIG DES MOLINS

Beside Dalt Vila stands Puig des Molins, the Hill of Windmills. Long before the windmills appeared, the hill was the largest necropolis of Carthaginian Ibiza. Several thousand tombs have already been found and excavated, and more almost certainly lie below the olive groves and flower-covered slopes. Many of the excavated finds from the necropolis, and from that at Es Cuieram at the northeastern tip of the island, are exhibited in the Museu Puig des Molins in Via Romana, which runs along the bottom of the hill.

Outside the museum there is a marked walkway through the necropolis.

One excavated site can be visited. It is known as the Mule Hypogea because it was found when a mule fell down the old tomb in 1946. Hypogea is the name given to the Carthaginian method of interring the dead, one excavation containing a number of side chambers in which sarcophagi or cremated remains were placed.

✚ *Eivissa 1d (off map)* ✉ 31 Via Romana ☎ 971 30 17 71 🕔 Museum: Apr–Sep Tue–Sat 10–2, 6–8, Sun 10–2; Oct–Mar Tue–Sat 9–3, Sun 10–2 🖐 Free 🍴 Bon Profit (€) in Plaça des Parc (➤ 91)

SA PENYA

At the far end of the harbour from Eivissa's new town, crammed into the narrow strip of land between Dalt Vila and the sea, is Sa Penya, one of the oldest sections of the town to lie outside the medieval walls. Today Sa Penya is Eivissa's main gypsy quarter, one of the islands' poorest areas, and has a less than salubrious reputation. But it's also Ibiza's gay village, with a couple of dozen bars on Carrer de la Verge alone.

Traditionally, Sa Penya was the fishermen's quarter of Eivissa and though there's a handsome old fish market, the Mercat des Peix, on Carrer Manuel Sora, it's rarely open these days. Sa Penya slumbers during the day, only coming to life after the heat of the sun has relented. A tour is often interrupted by lines of drying washing, fast-moving children or dogs. Yet there is an excitement and reality about Sa Penya that is sometimes absent from the glossier shopping streets just a stone's throw away.

To experience Sa Penya at its best, follow Carrer d'Enmig (the aptly named street in the middle) from Plaça d'Antoni Riguer (go up Calle Pou then turn second left) to Plaça de Sa Riba at the harbour's end. Running parallel, one street further from the sea, is Carrer de la Verge (also known as Carrer Mare de Deu – Mother of God Street), with some of the oldest houses in Eivissa.

✚ *Eivissa 3c* 🍴 For lunch El Faro (€€; ➤ 91), on the harbourfront; for a budget dinner El Pirata (€) or Pasajeros (€; both ➤ 92)

SANT DOMÈNEC

Positioned between the Baluard de Santa Llúcia and Plaça d'Espanya, Sant Domènec is immediately recognizable by its delightful red-tiled cupolas. Inside there are 19th-century frescoes, restored after a disastrous fire all but destroyed them.

🚼 *Eivissa 3d* ✉ Between Baluard de Santa Llúcia and Plaça d'Espanya 🖐 Free access 🍴 La Torreta (€€; ➤ 92), Plaça de la Vila, near the Portal de ses Taules

HOTELS

Casa de Huéspedes Vara de Rey (€)
Modest but charming little place in a period town house right in the heart of town. Many rooms are on the small side and do not have private bathrooms, but all have character.
✉ 7 Passeig de Vara de Rey ☎ 971 30 13 76; www.hibiza.com
🕐 Easter–Oct

Hostal Parque (€€)
Renovated in 2007, this is a stylish hotel with contemporary decor and an enviable location. There's a café on the ground floor.
✉ 4 Plaça des Parc ☎ 971 30 13 58; www.hostalparque.com 🕐 All year

El Hotel (€€€)
Eivissa's hippest hotel, owned by the club Pacha (► 61), which stands opposite. Cutting-edge design throughout, and there's a fab restaurant and bar, though the pool area is disappointingly small.
✉ Passeig Marítim ☎ 971 31 59 63; www.elhotelpacha.com 🕐 All year

La Marina (€€)
Pleasant and occasionally funky modern en-suite rooms attached to a harbourfront restaurant. All rooms have air conditioning, and many have balconies.
✉ 7 Carrer Barcelona ☎ 971 31 01 72; www.hostal-lamarina.com 🕐 All year

Mirador de Dalt Vila (€€€)
Exclusive Relais & Chateaux-accredited hotel in a Dalt Vila palace, opened in 2007. Chic modern rooms are furnished with antiques, there's a superb restaurant, and extras include yacht charter.
✉ 4 Plaça d'Espanya, Dalt Vila ☎ 971 30 30 45; www.hotelmiradoribiza.com
🕐 All year

Los Molinos (€€€)
Located by the coast in Figueretes, this comfortable hotel has good facilities, including a large pool set in palm-filled gardens.
✉ 60 Carrer Ramón Muntaner ☎ 971 30 22 50; www.thbhotels.com
🕐 All year

Montesol (€€)

An atmospheric, if rather musty, old colonial-style hotel, as close to the heart of town as it gets. However, facilities are limited and traffic noise is an issue.

✉ Passeig de Vara de Rey ☎ 971 31 01 61; www.hotelmontesol.com
🕐 All year

El Puerto (€€)

Unexciting but well-priced large hotel that's close to La Marina and Passeig de Vara de Rey. Has a pool and apartments.

✉ 22 Carrer de Carlos III ☎ 971 31 38 12; www.ibizaelpuerto.com
🕐 All year

Royal Plaza (€€€)

Large modern business hotel near the centre of town. Excellent facilities, including a rooftop pool with great views of Dalt Vila.

✉ 27–29 Carrer Pedro Francés ☎ 971 31 37 11; www.hotelroyalplaza.net
🕐 All year

Sol y Brisa (€)

A humble yet clean little family-owned pension, on a quiet street. Some rooms have showers, all have air conditioning and fridges.

✉ Avinguda Bartomeu Vincent Ramon ☎ 971 31 08 18 🕐 All year

La Torre del Canónigo (€€€)

Classy hotel in a restored 14th-century tower close to the cathedral. Huge rooms and spectacular views of the port area.

✉ 8 Carrer Mayor, Dalt Vila ☎ 971 30 38 84; www.elcanonigo.com
🕐 Easter–Oct

La Ventana (€€€)

Art-filled, elegant converted town house beautifully furnished with antiques – some rooms even have four-poster beds. Great views of the harbour from the roof terrace, which has a bar and is a great place to take an aperitif in the early evening.

✉ 13 Sa Carrossa, Dalt Vila ☎ 971 39 08 57; www.laventana.com
🕐 All year

RESTAURANTS

Alfredo's (€€)

Ibiza's oldest restaurant (dating from 1934), decorated with photos of the island before the tourist boom. Specializes in Spanish and Ibizan cooking. Mixed grills of fish and meat are a revelation, and the speciality 'black rice', made with sepia, is delicious.

✉ 16 Passeig de Vara de Rey ☎ 971 31 12 74 🕐 Tue–Sat 1–5pm, 8pm–1am, Sun 1–5

Bon Profit (€)

Hugely popular place that serves Spanish comfort food in modern canteen-like surrounds. Be prepared to queue as no reservations are accepted.

✉ 5 Plaça des Parc 🕐 Daily 1–3, 8–10

La Brasa (€€€)

Located between Plaça des Parc and La Marina, this is one of the most attractive restaurants in Eivissa, with an atmospheric interior and the loveliest courtyard garden in town.

✉ 3 Pere Sala ☎ 971 30 12 02 🕐 Mon–Sat 1–5pm, 8pm–1am, Sun 1–5

El Corsario (€€)

The Spanish and Mediterranean cuisine may be dated, but there's no faulting the million-dollar view of the harbour you can enjoy from the terrace.

✉ 5 Poniente, Dalt Vila ☎ 971 30 12 48 🕐 Easter–Oct daily 8pm–midnight

Croissant Show (€)

An Eivissa institution that's as famous for buttery French pastries and quiches as for post-club revellers wanting a caffeine or fresh juice pick-me-up.

✉ Plaça de la Constitució ☎ 971 31 76 65 🕐 Daily 6am–5am

El Faro (€€)

Fish and shellfish on an elegant terrace at the harbour. The grouper and dorada are house specials.

✉ 4 Plaça Garijo ☎ 971 31 32 33 🕐 Easter–Sep daily 1pm–1am

Macao (€€)

Right at the eastern end of the harbour, this Italian restaurant has an imaginative menu with a few twists. The vibe is easy-going rather than formal.

✉ Plaça de sa Riba, Sa Penya ☎ 971 31 47 07 🕐 Easter–Sep daily 8pm–1am

Pasajeros (€)

An authentic local eatery beloved by a young clientele for its low prices, cosy dining rooms and informal atmosphere. It provides tasty home-style cooking.

✉ Carrer Vicent Soler, La Marina ☎ No phone 🕐 Daily 7pm–1am

El Pirata (€)

Enjoy tasty thin-crust pizzas from an Italian-owned pizzeria on the harbourfront of La Marina. It provides take-away as well as table service.

✉ 10b Carrer Garijo, La Marina ☎ 971 19 26 30 🕐 Daily 7pm–1am

Plaza del Sol (€)

Sitting pretty above the port area, this popular place by the Portal Nou has a wonderful terrace virtually on top of the old city walls. The menu concentrates on Spanish and Mediterranean classics.

✉ Plaça del Sol, Dalt Vila ☎ 971 39 07 73 🕐 Easter–Sep daily 1–3pm, 8:30pm–1am

La Torreta (€€)

Possibly the finest restaurant in Plaça de la Vila. People come for gourmet French and Spanish food. Eat on the terrace or inside.

✉ Plaça de la Vila ☎ 971 30 04 11 🕐 Daily 7pm–midnight

El Zaguan (€)

Ever-popular, spacious, modern tapas bar a block across from Passeig de Vara de Rey. There's a large menu of daily specials or you can help yourself from the bar – bills are charged by the number of cocktail sticks on your plate.

✉ 15 Bartolome de Roselló ☎ 971 192 882 🕐 Daily 12–12

SHOPPING

CRAFTS
Artisana Ibicenca-Alfareria
Island ceramics – from *sangria* jugs to sculptural folk figures.
✉ 16 Carrer Aragón ☎ No phone

FASHION
The commercial shopping streets are Passeig de Vara de Rey and Avinguda Bartomeu Vincent Ramon, but the most interesting stores lie in the tangle of lanes at the west end of La Marina. Here are boutiques selling Ad Lib fashions, a bohemian Ibizan style that emerged in the hippy 1970s, with white, loose-flowing designs.

Ad Libitum
Classic Ad Lib fashions: all-white, floaty bohemian clothing.
✉ 10 Carrer Bisbe Cardona ☎ 971 31 06 54

Divina
Famous Ad Lib store specializing in flowing designs and classic details. Pretty children's clothes, too.
✉ 7 Carrer Santa Creu, Dalt Vila ☎ 971 30 08 15

Pacha
Cherry-branded merchandise – from clothing to bags via motorbike helmets – from the island's original superclub.
✉ 20 Carrer Tur i Palau ☎ 971 31 35 35; www.pacha.com

Sandal Shop
Superbly crafted, beautifully stylish handmade bags and belts. A second outlet on Passeig de Vara de Rey specializes in handbags.
✉ 2 Plaça de la Vila ☎ 971 30 54 75

MUSIC
Delta Discos
Clubbing anthems, flamenco, folk and Spanish pop in a music shop going strong since the late 1960s.
✉ 7 Avinguda d'Espanya ☎ 971 30 67 21; www.discosdeltaibiza.com

ENTERTAINMENT

BARS

Base Bar

Boasts a terrific harbourfront terrace ideal for people-watching.
Draws a young crowd (and a celebrity or two).
✉ 15 Carrer Garijo, La Marina 🕐 May–Oct 9pm–3:30am

Dôme

Near the old market, this is Eivissa's premier gay bar, clubby and at
its best when the club parades roll in.
✉ S/n Carrer Alfonso XII 🕐 May–Oct 10pm–4am

Rock Bar

Next to the Base Bar, but slightly less raucous than its neighbour.
It's popular as a venue for a final drink before hitting the clubs.
✉ 14 Carrer Garijo, La Marina 🕐 May–Oct 9:30pm–3:30am

Teatro Pereyra

Relaxed bohemian bar in a former theatre foyer. Popular with an
older crowd, it hosts live jazz every night in summer.
✉ 3 Carrer de Comte Rosselló 🕐 Jul–Sep daily 9am–5am; Oct–Jun
Mon–Sat 8am–4am

CLUBS

Anfora

Eivissa's only gay club, this small venue is in a historic building in
Dalt Vila. Musically it's all about club hits and classic pop anthems.
✉ 7 Carrer Sant Carles, Dalt Vila 🕐 Apr–Oct, Easter and New Year

El Divino

Classy house music in an intimate modern club in the marina – a
free boat shuttles from the harbourfront.
✉ S/n Paseo de Juan Carlos I ☎ 971 19 01 76; www.eldivino-ibiza.com
🕐 Jun–Sep 11pm–6am

Pacha

See page 61.

Around Ibiza

Santa Eulària des Riu
(Santa Eulalia del Rio)

□ Sant Antoni de Portmany
(San Antonio Abad)

Just as there are several faces to Eivissa, there are several Ibizas, each distinctly different. The island packs into its diminutive size a range of landscapes and villages that appeal to everyone. From supermodels to escapist bohemians, young clubbers to families on a beach holiday, every visitor discovers an idyllic corner.

Most visitors stick to the coasts. Mass tourism has done its worst at places like Sant Antoni and Cala Llonga. Yet even here, beautiful coves lie 10 minutes' drive away. The southwest has morphed into a hipsters' playground at Ses Salines and Cala Jondal, while the little-developed, pine-cloaked north and west of the island hold vestiges of the hippy movement.

Inland Ibiza is another world again. Villages of white-cube houses lie scattered in the rust-red soils. Some, like Santa Getrudis or Sant Josep, have become bohemian bolt-holes that are developing fast as administrative centres. Others, like Santa Agnès and Sant Mateu, hold true to the rustic heritage of the island.

BALÀFIA

Approach Balàfia from the hamlet of Sant
Llorenç, little more than a cluster of
houses, a whitewashed 18th-century
church and the exceptional restaurant
La Paloma (➤ 59). From here it's 2km
(1.2 miles) to Balàfia itself, a village defined
by a crop of stone defence towers dating
back to Moorish times. The village is
reached by a dirt track off the main road,
opposite Cana Pepeta restaurant. For
much of Ibiza's history the island was
targeted by pirates, and the inhabitants
would shelter in Balàfia's towers in times
of trouble. Ignore the *privado* signs, which
refer to the land around the tiny village,
and take a stroll around the cobbled lanes,
admiring the North African-style flat-roofed
houses with their whitewashed exteriors.
Just south of the village is the restaurant
Camí de Balàfia (tel: 971 32 50 19), famous
for its grilled meats.

🕂 19J 🖾 West of the Eivissa–Portinatx road
🖐 Free 🍴 Camí de Balàfia 🚌 Eivissa–Portinatx

CALA BENIRRÀS

This beautiful pine-cloaked bay is one of
the loveliest beaches in the north of Ibiza.
Spared development except for a trio of
restaurants and fishermen's shacks, its
fjord-like notch in the cliffs provides a
broad sand beach and crystal-clear waters.
That it is more relaxed than other beaches
in the area means Benirràs is a neutral

ground for Ibiza's disparate tribes: families, clubbers and hippies, some of whom gather occasionally to play bongos at sunset.

➕ 18L ✉ 3km (2 miles) northeast of Port de Sant Miquel

🍴 Restaurant Benirràs (€€)

CALA D'HORT

Best places to see, pages 36–37.

CALA LLENYA

In the northeast of Ibiza, close to the village of Sant Carles, there are three delightful beaches: Cala Mastella (➤ 98), Cala Boix and Cala Llenya. Of these, Cala Llenya has by far the best sands, ideal for children, and you'll also find pedalos for hire. The pretty bay is backed by low cliffs, and with no large resorts in the vicinity, Cala Llenya never gets too packed. There's just one efficient *chiringuito* here, which rustles up *tostadas* and snacks at fair prices.

➕ 22J ✉ 4km (2.5 miles) east of Sant Carles 🖐 Free 🍴 *Chiringuito* on the beach 🚌 16 from Santa Eulària

CALA LLONGA

Before mass tourism, Cala Llonga was one of the scenic highlights of the island. Then the developers came, building apartments and hotels, boosting the local economy but not adding to the scenic delights of the bay. On the positive side, the sheltered beach is one of the best on the island for children.

Also, the southern edge of Cala Llonga, as far as Cap des Llibrell, has been designated an ANEI, an area of special interest, for its natural beauty, flowers and wildlife.

➕ 11E ✉ 3km (2 miles) south of Santa Eulària 🚌 Reached by buses from either Eivissa or Santa Eulària

CALA MASTELLA

There is a beach at Cala Mastella, but it is small – 50m (165ft) long and 10m (33ft) wide – so many swimmers use the rocks at the bay's edges, or the wall of the tiny port, as their platform. The waters here are clear and clean, the whole bay a delight, not least because development has been kept to a minimum and the relatively difficult access keeps visitor numbers within manageable limits.

Most of those who come will be heading for the bay's open-air café/bar, El Bigotes – follow the well-worn path across the rocks on the bay's left side. The curious name derives from the *bigotis* – moustache – of the owner, Joan Ferrer. Señor Ferrer's boat is moored in Mastella's little port as he is a fisherman as well as a cook, although duties have passed to his family nowadays. In high season it's essential to reserve a day or more in advance for this delightful restaurant. The menu here is simplicity itself, usually *bullit de peix*, an incomparable fish stew.

➕ 22J ✉ From the centre of Sant Carles, take the road signposted for Cala Llenya and Cala Mastella 🍴 El Bigotes (➤ 131; €€)
🚌 Not on a bus route

CALA SALADA

A niche on the western coastline, Cala Salada is a gorgeous sandy beach a short

distance north of Sant Antoni. The beach is
small but peaceful, as there's been no
tourism development – the only buildings
here are a few luxury villas and a good
beachside restaurant. It's possible to walk
via the fishermen's huts (or swim) to a
second tiny beach, Ses Fontanelles, just
across the bay. Sunset views are sublime
here, when the sun sinks into the ocean
behind the offshore islets of Sa Conillera
and Bosc.

✚ 14H ✉ 4km (2.5 miles) north of Sant Antoni
🍴 Restaurant Cala Salada (€€), right on the beach
🚌 Not on a bus route

CALA VEDELLA

Many believed Vedella was Ibiza's most
beautiful cove before the coming of mass
tourism, but recent development that has
reached down to the beach has done little
for its looks. Nevertheless, with its
sheltering headlands, extremely fine-grained
sand and amazingly clear water, Cala Vedella
is excellent for swimming and there are
good facilities, both at the beach and in the
small resort area to the rear. Water-sports
equipment can be hired, and the bars and
restaurants are especially good. The cove is
a fine natural harbour and there are ample
opportunities for boat trips – some going as
far as Formentera.

✚ 2D ✉ North of Cala d'Hort, reached by road
from Cala d'Hort or Sant Josep 🚌 Bus 26
from Eivissa

CALA XARRACA

Cala Xarraca is a tiny half-moon bay cut into the inner arc of a much larger cove, one enclosed by the headlands of Punta sa Torre near Portinatx, and Xarraca to the west. There's a peaceful sand-and-shingle beach, a fairly humble beachside bar-restaurant and a couple of tiny coves just west of the main beach. About 1km (0.6 miles) to the east, you'll find another idyllic cove, Cala Xucla, which has its own *chiringuito* (Jun–Sep only).

✚ 19M ⊠ Beside a sharp bend of the C733 ⑪ Cala Xarraca (➤ 131; €) 🚌 Bus 20 on the Eivissa–Portinatx route

ES CANAR

Es Canar is a brash modern resort town aimed at British and German tourists. As a link with its past, there is a tiny harbour where fishing boats are moored while their owners dry nets.

The town lies on the northern side of the headland of Punta Arabí (➤ 112–113) and a fine two-hour walk from Es Canar follows the coast around Punta Arabí and down to Santa Eulària (➤ 50–51).

The beach of Es Canar curves round from the centre, its sands covered with sunbeds and parasols, and the waters of the bay are completely current-free, making it one of the safest on Ibiza for children. It is possible to hire all kinds of water-sports equipment here, or to join a boat trip around the coast.

Cala Nova, a kilometre (0.6 miles) north from Es Canar, offers more space and finer sands.

✚ 22H ⊠ 5km (3 miles) from Santa Eulària. Take the road to Sant Carles, forking right along a road that runs through pine woods ⑪ Mar Bella (€€), behind the beach 🚌 Bus 18 from Santa Eulària; also served by discobuses

ES CUBELLS

The road to Es Cubells from Sant Josep passes through fine countryside, the fields planted at intervals with olives and vines. It is an attractive little village studded with stands of pine trees and has a collection of luxurious island homes perched above the coast.

Within the village an old monastery has been converted into a school, while a theological college stands high on a rocky outcrop. To complete this scene of piety there is a fine village church.

From Es Cubells a road runs high above the cliffs towards the headland of Cap Llentrisca, and on to Cala d'Hort (➤ 36–37).

✚ 4B 🍴 Bar Llumbi, beside the church on the main square (€; closed Mon)

🚌 Bus 42 from Eivissa, though there are only irregular services

a drive around Northeast Ibiza

This drive follows Ibiza's western coast before turning
inland through wonderful scenery to reach the main
island road.

*From Eivissa take the E10, signposted Santa Eulària,
Portinatx, then bear right along the road signposted
Jesús. Continue through the village and, after 5km
(3 miles), pass the golf course. After a further 4km
(2.5 miles), bear right at the turn to Cala Llonga (➤ 97).*

*Go through Santa Eulària (➤ 50–51), following the
road signposted Sant Carles, ignoring the right fork for*

*Es Canar. After 8km (5 miles), in
Sant Carles (San Carlos), turn left at
the T-junction, following the road
signposted Cala de Sant Vicent.
After about 6km (4 miles), as you
near Sant Vicent, the sign of a
camera at the roadside indicates a
good viewpoint (although there is
no parking place other than the
road itself, which can be a
dangerous place to linger).*

The road reaches a T-junction.

Turn right here for a short detour and lunch at Es Calo
restaurant, in Cala de Sant Vicent.

*The route turns to the left, signposted Sant Joan,
Portinatx. After 3km (2 miles) turn right along a narrow
road, signposted Sant Vicent. Bear left past the church
and follow a single-track road, bearing left by the sports
court to rejoin the main road at a T-junction. Turn right.*

*After 6km (4 miles) you reach Sant Joan de Labritja (San
Juan). Continue through the town and, after a further
2km (1.2 miles), take the road that is signposted Eivissa.
Follow the main road for 15km (9 miles), passing Balàfia
(▶ 96) on the right, to reach a roundabout. Go straight
across, signposted Eivissa, following the main road for
a further 8km (5 miles) to reach a roundabout on the
outskirts of Eivissa.*

Distance 65km (40 miles)
Time 6 hours
Start/end point Eivissa ✚ 9C
Lunch Es Calo (€€) ✉ Cala de Sant Vicent ☎ 971 32 01 40

MIRADOR DEL SAVINAR

From the parking spot just off the Cala d'Hort–Es Cubells road, walk along the track to reach a broad area of cliff top. To the left from here a steep and somewhat vague path climbs to the object of the walk – the old watchtower overlooking Isla Vedrà. It is one of

the best preserved on the coast. Follow the path with care; the combination of polished rocks and windblown sand – the latter acting like ball bearings – means the ascent is slippery.

Some maps of Ibiza show the tower marked as Torre des Savinar, others as Torre d'en Pirata. It was built in the 18th century as a lookout for pirates approaching Ibiza's southern shore. Lookout towers are known as *talaias* in *Eivissenc*, an interesting name as the island's highest peak is known as Sa Talaia. Presumably at one stage it, too, was used as a watchtower.

The towers were constructed all around the island within sight of each other so a beacon fire lit at one could rapidly pass a danger signal to all the islanders.

From the tower the eye is drawn to Es Vedrà, home, legend has it, of the Sirens who lured sailors to their doom in Homer's story of Odysseus (Ulysses). The island is one of the most famous of all Ibizan landmarks, seen on hundreds of postcards. It is at its most picturesque when viewed from here, where its sheer cliffs are seen rising above the smaller island of Es Vedranell.

➕ 2B ✉ Take the road for Cala d'Hort and turn along a dirt track downhill and around to the left – it should be signed Torre des Savinar, although an access dispute means it may not. The dirt track to Sa Pedrera, off the same road, also has paths leading off it to the tower. Parking is possible on both these tracks close to the road; further on the tracks become rougher 🍴 Es Boldado (➤ 131; €€)

NUESTRA SEÑORA DE JESÚS
Best places to see, pages 44–45.

PLATJA DE SES SALINES
Best places to see, pages 48–49.

PORT DE SANT MIQUEL

This deep-cut inlet on the northern coast is an excellent natural
harbour and has a white sand beach. On the eastern side there are
several large concrete hotels – the Hotel Clubs Cartago, Galeon
and San Miquel. Steps up to these offer excellent platforms for
photographers wanting shots of the bay.

Beyond the hotels is the **Cova de Can Marçà,** a cavern once
used by smugglers. Excavations have revealed animal bones,
mostly of rodents, but no firm evidence for occupation by man.
Today the cave is open to the public, and a rather kitsch son-et-
lumière show has been added to the natural beauty of the

stalagmites and
stalactites. Beyond the
cave, the road continues to
the beautiful Cala Benirràs
(➤ 96). About 3km
(2 miles) west of Port de
Sant Miquel is the five-star Hacienda Na Xamena (➤ 130).

 18L ✉ 4km (2.5 miles) north of the village of Sant Miquel

Cova de Can Marçà

✉ Port de Sant Miquel ☎ 971 33 47 76 🕙 May–Oct daily 10:30–1:30,
2:30–8; Nov–Apr 11–5:30 ✋ Expensive

PORT DES TORRENT

This old village/port is now little
more than a brash, touristy
overflow of Sant Antoni de
Portmany (▶ 116–117), though the
small beach is pleasant and the
rocks on its western edge offer a
good walk.

To the west of Port des Torrent
is Cala Bassa, a short bus ride from
Sant Antoni. Although usually very
busy, it is a beautiful bay with a
beach more than 200m (220yds)
long hemmed in by steep cliffs
whose bases offer excellent
snorkelling. For more peace, follow
the path from the road end,
heading inland at first, but then
curving with the bay to reach the
cliff top at its western edge. From
here there is a fine view towards
Sant Antoni. The next bay is Cala
Roja, on the western headland of
which is a watchtower. From the
tower there is an impressive view
across the sea to Sa Conillera. In
Ibizan legend, Conillera was the
birthplace of Hannibal. There is a
sheltered harbour and regular
boats trips from Sant Antoni.

✚ 4E ✉ On the western outskirts of
Sant Antoni 🍴 Restaurant Cala Bassa
(€€) 🚌 Buses 2 and 6 from Sant Antoni
to Port des Torrent

EXPLORING

PORTINATX

The village of Portinatx (pronounced 'Port-e-natch') represents a happy medium in tourism terms: enough development to support the local economy, but not so overpowering that the essential beauty of the place is destroyed. Though there are tourist hotels and apartments, there is still a fringe of pine and juniper to Portinatx's beautiful half-moon cove, famed for its shallow waters, where many ships were able to ride out a storm. The defence tower on the western side of the headland is a good objective for a walk, as is the eastern side of the bay, with a path hugging the cliff edge all the way to Punta Moscarter.

Those looking for equally fine views, but of the cliffs rather than from them, can hire boats at Portinatx. A boat trip westwards, passing Cala Xarraca (➤ 100) to reach the very remote coast near Cap Blanc, is especially rewarding.

✚ 20M ✉ Northern tip of Ibiza, at the end of the main C733 road from Eivissa 🍴 Cas Mallorqui (€€) 🚌 Bus 20 from Eivissa; 21 from Santa Eulària

PUIG DE MISSA

This curious little hill stands on the western outskirts of Santa Eulària (➤ 50–51), the church at its top accessible by a steep, winding road, or by following the pink-signed *paisatge pirtoresc* (picturesque path) which climbs up in about 15 minutes. The

hill itself is charming for its church and houses that top it, but is chiefly visited for the view it offers of the town and local coastline. Try to visit during the evening when the softer, orange-tinged light creates a magical view of Santa Eulària and the hilltop buildings. Below the church is a restored house containing the Museu Etnològic d'Eivissa i Formentera. This museum has an important collection of traditional costumes, agricultural tools (including a colossal olive press) and the odd curio, such as a framed corsair's licence.

➕ 20H ⏱ Museum: Apr–Sep Mon–Sat 10–2, 5:30–8, Sun 11–1:30; Oct–Mar Tue–Sat 10–2, Sun 11–1:30 ✋ Moderate 🍴 Ca Na Ribes (€€; ➤ 133) 🚌 Eivissa–Santa Eulària; the bus does not go to the top of the hill

PUNTA ARABÍ

Punta Arabí is little more than a string of modern tourism development that straggles alongside the road south of Es Canar. Yet in the 1960s, with the rise of Flower Power and hippy culture, this uninspiring area was the cradle of a youthful Utopia as the host of Ibiza's first hippy market. While hippies in the USA congregated on the west coast of California, in Europe the wellspring of counterculture was Ibiza. Franco's Spain was not the most liberal country in Europe, far from it in fact, but Ibiza was an island a long way off. Franco's repressions caused major waves in Madrid, but by the time the waves had reached Ibiza they were minor ripples. There was another factor, too. The Ibizans were a cosmopolitan people, and were philosophical about new settlers.

Bohemian travellers first settled in the Sant Carles area in the early 1960s. Hippy markets have been around since that time, and the weekly event at Club Punta Arabí (Wednesdays) was one of the original sites. Today it's far more commercialized, and many of the goods are mass-produced Asian imports – the market at Las Dalias (➤ 69) is more authentic.

➕ 22H ✉ Just south of Es Canar 🚌 Bus 18 from Santa Eulària

a walk to Punta Arabí

From the marina in Santa Eulària it's simple to follow Ibiza's glorious eastern coastline up to the promontory of Punta Arabí.

The path loops past sandy beaches, and winds past villas, but never strays too far from the shoreline, so it's impossible to get lost.

You first pass a new modernist convention centre, where concerts are held, before tracking past Cala Niu Blau (Blue Nest Beach), which has a good fish restaurant.

Continuing northeast, you'll pass the beach-facing gardens of some expensive villas and then come to Cala Pada.

Cala Pada has a sandy beach with good *chiringuitos*, safe swimming and boat connections back to Santa Eulària and on to Es Canar.

Next up is S'Argamassa, a small upmarket beach resort, before the path heads inland for a minute or two to loop around the wooded Punta Arabí peninsula.

If it's a Wednesday, you could make a diversion to Club Punta Arabí, where there's a large hippy market (➤ 69, 111).

*Otherwise it's less than 1km (0.6 miles) to Es Canar,
from where there are boats and buses back to
Santa Eulària.*

Distance 6km (4 miles)
Time 2 hours
Start point Santa Eulària marina ✚ 21H
End point Es Canar ✚ 22H
Lunch Brisa del Mar, Cala Pada (€€) ☎ 971 33 08 26

SA CALETA

In the history of Ibiza, Sa Caleta is famous as one of the two original Phoenician sites on the island, the other being at Eivissa. Phoenician Sa Caleta, however, was inhabited for as little as 40 years or so, until around 600BC, and seems never to have been much more than a settlement peopled by fishermen and their families. When it was abandoned, all Phoenician interest in Ibiza was concentrated in Eivissa.

Today Sa Caleta is a delightful cove, its picturesque red cliffs and shallow turquoise sea enhanced by the scattering of fishermen's huts. To the west is the curious headland of Punta des Jondal, a skeletal finger of rock poking out into the Mediterranean. The rock of the headland and Fita des Jondal, the hillock which separates Sa Caleta from Cala Jondal, is a beautiful golden brown, a fine contrast with the green pines that top the cliffs and the clear blue waters. Cala Jondal itself is popular despite its apparent isolation and in recent years has emerged as one of the island's hippest beaches due to beach clubs like Blue Marlin. It has pebbles as well as sand, and good restaurants set among large coastal pines.

➕ 6B ✉ Signposted from the main Eivissa–Sant Josep highway

🍽 Restaurante Sa Caleta (€€)

SANTA AGNÈS DE CORONA

Santa Agnès de Corona (Santa Inés) is one of the most remote villages on Ibiza. Set among the uplands known as Es Amunts and close to the most inhospitable part of the coast, the village has retained its Ibizan character.

The setting is wonderful, with the peak of Puig d'en Serra just to the south, and the village is approached between almond orchards, the trees growing in startling red-brown soil.

The church, built in the early years of the last century, stands in the main square. On the wall facing the village square is a statue of an Agnus Dei, or Lamb of God, perhaps a play on the village saint's name. Here you will find a few concessions to modern Ibiza – a great café/bar and a few local crafts for sale.

From close to the village, dirt roads head for the coast and towards the hills. On the coast the rugged cliffs around Cap Negret offer spectacular views (especially to the islands of Ses Margalides) as you walk the coastal path, though care is needed as the path is very rocky and the cliffs here are among the highest on the island.

North of the village the coast towards Cap des Mossons is as remote as it gets on the island. If you are tempted this way be sure to have good walking boots and a good supply of water.

➕ 15J ✉ One of the most picturesque drives in Ibiza heads northwards from Sant Antoni along a road which runs parallel to the coast to reach Sant Miquel. The first village along this road – a short detour off the road is required – is Santa Agnès 🍽 Can Cosmi (€), on the main square 🚌 Bus 30, which runs between Eivissa and Sant Antoni

SANT ANTONI DE PORTMANY

Sant Antoni de Portmany (San Antonio Abad), Ibiza's second-largest town, could hardly be more different from Eivissa. Yet for all its brash modernity, it is an historically interesting town, one whose development mirrors the development of the island.

Perhaps because of the existence of an early chapel, just north of Sant Antoni bay, in 1305 the Bishop of Tarragon gave permission for the construction of a church and consecrated cemetery in Sant Antoni. That church, on Plaça de l'Església, dedicated to St Anthony and so giving the town its name, is one of the oldest in

Ibiza. Built on the site of a Moorish mosque, it incorporates some architectural details it presumably borrowed from its predecessor, as well as the more typical fortress-like looks of its day.

For many years Sant Antoni was a fishing port, and one link with those days can be found at Cala Gració a little way to the north. There the Cova de ses Llegostes, a natural fish pool, was used by the local fishermen to keep excess fish fresh while they waited for market. Today the cave has been turned into a natural **aquarium.**

Sant Antoni developed into a small town in the 1960s and 1970s. Virtually overnight the town was transformed into the island's major package-holiday centre, as hotel and apartment blocks arose around the fine harbour, together with bars, discos and souvenir shops.

In the 1980s Sant Antoni's reputation sank to an all-time low as the resort developed a reputation as a hotbed of lager louts and drunken excess, but in recent years a number of initiatives to shift upmarket have injected life and vitality into the town. An elegant new promenade now graces the western half of Sant Antoni, and a number of hip bar-restaurants have been built, forming a stylish zone called the Sunset Strip. 'San An' remains the bastion of young British holidaymakers, complete with the excesses of its infamous bar-strip, the 'West End', around Carrer Sant Agnès. Avoid this area in high season and you'll find it an unpretentious, boisterous resort.

➕ 14G ✉ 16km (10 miles) from Eivissa, at the other end of the C731 🍴 Es Rebost de Can Prats (€€; ➤ 132) 🚌 Very regular services, including bus 3 (Eivissa–Sant Rafel–Sant Antoni), which leaves every 15 mins at peak times

Aquarium Cap Blanc

✉ Cova de ses Llegostes, Cala Gració 🕐 Apr–Sep daily 10–7 💶 Moderate 🍴 Novedad (€€), Cala Gració

SANT CARLES DE PERALTA

The beautiful little market town of Sant Carles de Peralta (San Carlos) is set among some of Ibiza's most idyllic scenery.

The area around town is almost a study in contrasts. To the south, close to the road, is a collection of ruinous buildings and tall cylindrical chimneys, the remains of old lead mines first dug by the Carthaginians. Closer to the town, the rich red earth, wonderfully fertile despite the relative lack of water, is intensively farmed. In Sant Carles itself, the centrepiece is the church, notorious for the death of the curate in still mysterious circumstances during the Civil War. Built in the 18th century, it is more graceful than many others on the island and has a beautiful double-arcaded entrance. At first glance it could be mistaken for an elegant country house: only when the simple bell housing and cross on the roof are seen does the building's true nature become clear.

In the 1960s Ibiza was 'invaded' by hippies who set up market stalls at places on the coast near Sant Carles. As time passed many of the hippies migrated inland, some arriving in the town. Their wilder days over, some have settled down, adding a vitality (there are several boutiques and good cafés) to the town which makes a visit even more enjoyable.

🚌 21J ✉ On the main road from Santa Eulària to the northeastern tip of the island 🍴 Bar Anita (€; ➤ 132), close to the church and full of character 🚌 Santa Eulària–Es Figueral

SANTA EULÀRIA DES RIU
Best places to see, pages 50–51.

SANTA GERTRUDIS

Best places to see, pages 52–53.

SANT JOAN DE LABRITJA

Sant Joan de Labritja (St John the Baptist) lies in one of Ibiza's most beautiful valleys, formed between the high peaks of the

Serra de la Mala Costa, to the south, and, to the north, hills that slope down to cliffs above remote bays such as Cala d'en Serra and Port de ses Caletes. The high point of the southern hills, Es Fornàs, is the third-highest Ibizan peak. A dirt track leads up to the peak from the road linking Sant Joan to Sant Vicent. It is a difficult drive and caution is needed, but the reward is a magnificent view over Ibiza's wild northeastern corner, and southwards towards Eivissa.

For such a small town – little more than a village – Sant Joan has a surprising number of banks, perhaps reflecting its position as the chief town of one of Ibiza's administrative districts. The Ajuntament – the former regional headquarters, now a café-restaurant – is a lovely building. Opposite is an unusual terrace of balconied houses. The village highlight is the colonnaded 18th-century church with its slim, distinctive steeple (a later addition) and tiled cupola.

✚ 20L ✉ 24km (15 miles) north of Eivissa, just off the C733 road to Portinatx
🍴 Café Vista Alegre (€€), 1 Calle de Eivissa 🚌 Bus 20 on the Eivissa–Portinatx route

SANT JOSEP

Sant Josep is in an elevated position on a hillside above a fertile plain, the surrounding hills covered in pines. Today more a small town than a village, it is developing rapidly, and significant numbers of visitors are drawn by the restaurants, craft shops and art galleries. Look, too, for shops selling embroidery, most of it made locally.

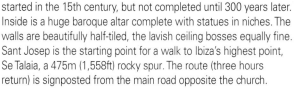

Also worth looking for is the church, a typically fortress-like building with an elegant arcaded entrance. The church was started in the 15th century, but not completed until 300 years later. Inside is a huge baroque altar complete with statues in niches. The walls are beautifully half-tiled, the lavish ceiling bosses equally fine. Sant Josep is the starting point for a walk to Ibiza's highest point, Se Talaia, a 475m (1,558ft) rocky spur. The route (three hours return) is signposted from the main road opposite the church.

✚ 4D ✉ Sant Josep is on the main highway in the southern part of the island, which connects Sant Antoni with Eivissa 🍽 El Destino (€€; ➤ 133)
🚌 Buses 8, 26 and 42 from Eivissa

SANT MIQUEL DE BALANSAT

Try to visit Sant Miquel de Balansat (San Miguel) on a late
Thursday afternoon when the square in front of the church hosts
performances of Ibizan folk dances to the music of an authentic
folk band (from 6pm). The meanings of most of the dances are
lost in time, but many seem to relate to courtship. Some of the
performers wear traditional costume, the men clothed in red

hats, bandannas and cummerbunds, black jackets and baggy white trousers, the women in long, black or white pleated skirts with aprons, long shawls and mantillas. The women also braid their hair and wear ornate gold necklaces showing a distinct Moorish influence. This colourful display ends with the passing of a *porrón* (wine vessel) for all to sample.

The fortress-like church is a fine 14th-century building, one of the oldest on the island, though the porch and patio are later. Inside, the 17th-century wall paintings in the Benirràs chapel have been restored. There's a perspective of the northern half of the island and its thickly wooded terrain from a viewpoint just outside the church courtyard.

✚ 18K ✉ About 4km (2.5 miles) from Eivissa a road branches left from the C733 (the road to Portinatx), passing through Santa Gertrudis to reach Sant Miquel and, beyond, Port de Sant Miquel 🍴 C'an Rei (€), opposite the church turning, for a basic lunch; La Luna Nell'Orto (€€), 50m beyond, for a romantic evening meal 🚌 Bus 33 from Eivissa

SANT RAFEL

Close to the centre of the island, Sant Rafel lies just off the main highway that connects Eivissa to Sant Antoni and is virtually equidistant between the two. Though there are no real sights in Sant Rafel, the village church is a graceful building, its lines reminiscent of mainland churches, and dates from the 18th century. It's perched slightly east of the high street, and offers a marvellous view of Dalt Vila.

Sant Rafel appeals to all visitors, but the attractions are quite diverse. Some come because the village is a centre for ceramics, and there are a couple of potters on the main street, west of the centre. Long after the potteries have closed the other major Sant Rafel attraction opens its doors. This is Privilege (► 61), the largest club in the world (according to the *Guinness Book of Records*) with a capacity approaching 10,000 people. With its internationally famous DJs, its swimming pool and amazing light shows, a visit to Privilege is a stunning experience.

🕇 8E ✉ Just north of the main C731 highway that links Eivissa with Sant Antoni 🍴 El Clodenis, an elegant Provençal restaurant next to the church 🚌 Eivissa–Sant Antoni buses pass through town

SERRA GROSSA

Technically, Serra Grossa refers to the island's largest area of unspoiled upland, which lies between the C731, the main highway linking Eivissa and Sant Antoni, and the road from Eivissa to Sant Josep. However, the following information applies equally well to the uplands south of Sant Joan and those near Sant Mateu.

The typical cover of Ibiza's upland areas is a forest of Aleppo pine, though the pine stands are sometimes interspersed with almond, fig, carob and olive. Aleppo pine has a very thin needle, making it easier to survive summer's hot sun, and so casts little shadow. Beneath it, therefore, numerous flowers and shrubs thrive, the most obvious being Mediterranean heath *(Erica multiflora)*. However, in places where natural or man-made fires have destroyed the forest and overgrazing has impoverished the soil, there are areas of 'degraded' forest where lavender, southern grape hyacinth and various other colourful plants bloom. Lower down the hillsides, where ancient cultivated terraces have been allowed to return to the wild, gladioli, chrysanthemums, grape hyacinths and poppies thrive.

🕇 6D

SES SALINES

Salt production is Ibiza's only true industry, and certainly the only one that is not connected to tourism. Ibizan salt is still highly prized, as it is very pure. The process is simple: the salt pans are situated below sea level and in May the sluices are opened to allow water in, and then shut. For the next three months or so the sun does the hard work, evaporating the water to leave a crust of shimmering white salt on the pan's clay floor. The salt is then dug out of the pan and loaded onto ships for export.

The Carthaginians and other early trading nations needed salt to preserve their food during long sea voyages. Interestingly, one of the chief customers of Ibizan salt today is the Faroe Islands, where it is still used to salt fish: both the production process and the final uses are unchanged after 2,500 years. Ibiza exports around 50,000 tons of salt annually.

🔲 7B ✉ Take the Sant Josep road out of Eivissa and follow the signs for Platja des Salines; you'll drive through the salt pans just before you reach the beach 🍴 Jockey Club (€€), Platja de ses Salines 🚌 Bus 11 from Eivissa

TALAMANCA

Talamanca beach's prime attraction is its location, just a couple of kilometres north of Eivissa, so all the capital's cosmopolitan restaurants, shops and nightlife are on your doorstep. But with wide, gently shelving sands that are ideal for children, this sheltered bay has all-round appeal anyway. The water can be murky by Ibizan standards, however.

At its southern end there are a couple of good bar-restaurants, while the northern fringes of the bay have a *chiringuito* famous for its mussels and the upmarket Sa Punta restaurant.

Buses do serve Talamanca, but the most enjoyable way to get here is via the regular boat services from the La Marina quarter of Eivissa.

🔲 9D ✉ 2km (1.2 miles) north of Eivissa 🍴 Flotante (€), Platja Talamanca 🚌 Buses from Eivissa ⛴ Boats from Eivissa

HOTELS

PORTINATX
La Ciguenya (€)
A mid-sized hotel, just off Portinatx's beach, where most of the well-presented rooms have sea views. There's a nice pool area, restaurant and a small gym.

✉ S'Arenal Petit ☎ 971 32 06 14; www.laciguenya.com ◷ May to mid-Oct

SANT ANTONI AREA
Hostal La Torre (€€)
This small, good-value place on an undeveloped rocky coast has wonderful westerly aspects, particularly at sunset. Rooms have a slightly bohemian feel about them.

✉ Cap Negret, 2km (1.2 miles) north of Sant Antoni ☎ 971 34 22 71; www.hostallatorre.com ◷ Mar–Nov

Pikes (€€€)
One of Ibiza's most celebrated agrotourism hotels, famous as the location for Wham!'s *Club Tropicana* video and Freddie Mercury's birthday. Popular with superstar DJs for sophisticated hedonism.

✉ 5km (3 miles) northeast of Sant Antoni ☎ 971 34 22 22; www.pikeshotel.com ◷ All year

Stella Maris Paraiso (€€)
This relaxed, family-friendly resort five minutes' walk from Cala Gració has several pools spread over a spacious site and excellent on-site facilities such as a supermarket and evening entertainment.

✉ Cala Gració, 1km (0.6 miles) north of Sant Antoni ☎ 971 34 06 00; wwwclubstellamaris.com ◷ May–early Oct

SANT CARLES AREA
Can Curreu (€€€)
Traditional *Ibicenco* architecture is married to relaxed modern style in a rural hotel that brings superbly efficient management to rustic tranquillity. There's a first-class restaurant, pool, spa and stables.

✉ 2km (1.2 miles) south of Sant Carles ☎ 971 33 52 80; www.cancurreu.com ◷ All year

Can Talaias (€€€)

Sitting high in the northern hills, this wonderful hotel is the former home of English actor Terry-Thomas, now run by his son. The views from the hotel terrace are some of Ibiza's most dramatic.

✉ 3km (2 miles) east of Sant Carles, on the road to Cala Boix ☎ 971 33 57 42; www.hotelcantalaias.com 🕒 Easter–Oct

SANTA EULÀRIA AREA

Agroturismo Xarc (€€)

A stylish rural hotel where the large rooms are decorated in rustic minimalism. Guests have free access to mountain bikes.

✉ Can Guasch, 4km (2.5 miles) north of Santa Eulària ☎ 971 33 91 78; www.agroxarc.es 🕒 Feb to just before Christmas

Ca's Català (€€)

A neat little English-owned hotel just west of the centre of Santa Eulària, with an attractive pool area and sun terrace. No children.

✉ Carrer del Sol, Santa Eulària ☎ 971 33 10 06; www.cascatala.com 🕒 May–Oct

Can Pere (€€€)

This fine country hotel, on a hilltop, is classy and tranquil. Air-conditioned rooms, a glorious pool area and a good restaurant.

✉ 4km (2.5 miles) south of Sant Eulària ☎ 971 19 66 00; www.canperehotel.com 🕒 All year

Hostal Rey (€)

Old-fashioned hotel near shops and the 'street of restaurants'. It's dated and basic but perfectly acceptable for the price.

✉ 17 Carrer Sant Josep, Santa Eulària ☎ 971 33 02 10 🕒 All year

SANTA GERTRUDIS AREA

Cas Gasí (€€€)

Peace and sophistication reign in a romantic spa-manor deep in rural Ibiza. Graceful decor and faultless service.

✉ S/n Camino Viejo de Sant Mateu, 3km (2 miles) west of Santa Gertrudis ☎ 971 19 77 00; www.casgasi.com 🕒 All year

SANT JOSEP AREA
Finca Can Xuxu (€€€)
A beautifully situated rural hotel, not far from Cala Tarida, with extensive grounds, a lovely pool and gardens and accommodation that has style and real rustic character.

✉ 3.5km (just over 2 miles) west of Sant Josep ☎ 971 80 15 84; www.canxuxu.com ☻ Apr–Oct

Hostal Cala Molí (€€)
Set above Ibiza's western coast, this enjoyable little hotel has good service standards and a small pool. It's located in a delightful, unspoiled coastal region.

✉ 1km (0.6 miles) south of Cala Molí ☎ 971 80 60 02; www.calamoli.com ☻ May–Oct

SANT MIQUEL AREA
Hacienda Na Xamena (€€€)
One of the island's most expensive and luxurious hotels, this bohemian five-star place has stupendous cliff-top views over the ocean, as well as a good spa and a renowned gastronomic restaurant (➤ 59).

✉ Near Port de Sant Miquel ☎ 971 33 45 00 ☻ Apr–Oct

TALAMANCA
Lux Isla (€€)
At the northern end of Talamanca beach, a stone's throw from the waves, is this small, smart, modern hotel, with wheelchair access and a café.

✉ 1 Carrer Josep Pla 1, Talamanca ☎ 971 31 34 69; www.luxisla.com ☻ All year

Ses Figueres (€€)
Right on Talamanca beach, this pleasant hotel, totally renovated in 2006, offers neat rooms with the bonus of sea views. There's also a popular restaurant.

✉ Platja de Talamanca ☎ 971 31 43 13; www.hotelsesfigueres.com ☻ May–Oct

RESTAURANTS

CALA BOIX
La Noria (€€)
Above a delightful cove, its terrace shaded by pine trees, this relaxed restaurant serves a variety of fish and rice specials, such as *bullit de peix* (fish stew).

✉ Cala Boix ☎ 971 33 53 97 🕐 Easter–Oct daily 12–4, 7–11

CALA GRACIONETA
El Chiringuito (€€)
Fine cooking, including some international dishes, but the real draw here is the location, at the rear of a magical little cove beach. At night the owners decorate the pine-cloaked setting with candles.

✉ Cala Gracioneta ☎ 971 34 83 38 🕐 May–Oct daily 10am–1am

CALA D'HORT
Es Boldado (€€)
Specializing in fresh fish and langoustines, the menu also includes plenty of local rice-based dishes and daily specials. The views of Es Vedrà island are unmatched.

✉ Cala d'Hort ☎ 626 49 45 37 🕐 Daily 1pm–midnight

CALA MASTELLA
El Bigotes (€€)
Surely the most romantic eating place in Ibiza. Fresh fish – caught that morning – in a rustic setting beside the lapping sea. Set menu, no choice. Book a table a day or more in advance, in person (no telephone bookings).

✉ Cala Mastella ☎ 971 39 33 60 🕐 Easter–Nov daily 12–6

CALA XARRACA
Cala Xarraca (€)
Wonderfully sited right on the beach, this bar/restaurant has great views and a straightforward, inexpensive menu of snacks and main courses.

✉ Cala Xarraca ☎ 971 33 33 65 🕐 Easter–Oct daily 12–12

ES CAVALLET
La Escollera (€€€)
This airy, upmarket *chiringuito* is renowned for its fish and seafood, though there are some options for meat eaters.
✉ At the northern end of Es Cavallet beach ☎ 971 39 65 72 🕐 Jun–Aug daily 1–5, 7–12; Sep–May 1–5

JESÚS
Bon Lloc (€)
A pleasant bar-cum-restaurant over the main road from the church compound. Inexpensive prices (a set meal is around €9).
✉ On the main road through Jesús ☎ 971 31 18 13 🕐 Daily 7am–midnight

SANT ANTONI
Es Rebost de Can Prats (€€)
Enjoy traditional home-cooking in a long-standing family-run restaurant in the old quarter. The antithesis of the brash resort.
✉ 4 Carrer Cervantes ☎ 971 34 62 52 🕐 Wed–Mon 1–4, 8–12

Rincón de Pepe (€)
An informal restaurant in the heart of Sant Antoni. The tapas menu really stands out, with myriad tasty options.
✉ 6 Carrer Sant Mateu ☎ 971 34 06 97 🕐 Daily 1–4, 8–12

Sa Capella (€€€)
Housed in an ancient (though never consecrated) chapel, this is one of Ibiza's most evocatively situated restaurants. Fine Spanish and Mediterranean cuisine, beautifully presented.
✉ Off roundabout on the Santa Agnès road from Sant Antoni, at km 0.5 ☎ 971 34 00 57 🕐 May–Oct daily 8pm–1am

SANT CARLES
Bar Anita (€)
A marvellously atmospheric leftover from Sant Carles's hippy era that remains a hub of the local community. Tapas on the terrace with a *hierbas* digestif is one of the classics of Ibiza.
✉ Sant Carles, close to the church ☎ 971 33 50 90 🕐 Daily 8am–midnight

SANTA EULÀRIA
Ca Na Ribes (€€)
Two sites in town, both specializing in typical Ibizan/Mediterranean cooking – lots of fish, meat and rice.

✉ Carrer Sant Jaume 67 and Carrer de Sant Vicent 36 ☎ 971 33 00 06 (for both venues) 🕐 Easter–Nov Thu–Tue 12–4, 6–12

Rincon de Pepe (€)
This pleasingly old-fashioned outpost on the town's 'restaurant strip' is renowned for its wide-ranging tapas menu.

✉ 53 Carrer de Sant Vicent ☎ 971 33 13 21 🕐 Daily 1–4, 7–12

SANTA GERTRUDIS AREA
Ama Lur (€€€)
By the roundabout 3km (2 miles) south of Santa Gertrudis, this Basque restaurant specializes in seafood, and is one of the classiest in Ibiza.

✉ On the road between Eivissa and Sant Miquel ☎ 971 31 45 54
🕐 Mid-Mar to mid-Nov Thu–Tue 8pm–midnight

Bar Costa (€)
An institution, this famous bar-restaurant has a sociable vibe and a good tapas menu.

✉ Plaça de l'Església ☎ 971 19 70 21 🕐 Open all day

SANT JOSEP AREA
El Destino (€€)
Close to the church, with a small terrace. El Destino is a great choice for vegetarians, with many excellent tapas dishes. Book ahead.

✉ Atalaya 15 ☎ 971 80 03 41 🕐 Apr–Oct Mon–Sat 1pm–1am

Es Galliner (€)
An informal, bohemian bar-restaurant as popular for a drink in its green-cobbled interior as for a reliably tasty meal from the *menu del día* on the terrace.

✉ Carrer del Ajuntament 4 ☎ 971 80 15 54 🕐 Daily 9am–midnight

SHOPPING

ART, CERAMICS AND OBJETS D'ART

Art i fang
Modern art plus superbly crafted jewellery and ceramics.

✉ Carrer Pere Escanellas 19, Sant Josep ☎ 971 80 16 98

Cerámica Kinoto
A master craftsman's work, mainly patterned plates and bowls with a blue or green glaze, plus Phoenician-inspired designs.

✉ Can Kinoto, Sant Rafel ☎ 971 19 82 62; www.cankinoto.com

Galeria Can Daifa
A kind of gallery-garden, this delightful place sells paintings, mirrors and pottery. A €2 charity donation is requested.

✉ Near Plaça de l'Església, Santa Gertrudis ☎ 971 19 70 42

Galeria Es Molí
Arguably Ibiza's most renowned gallery, with an extensive choice of classic and contemporary art.

✉ On the Sant Miquel road from Eivissa, at km 1.3 ☎ 971 31 28 35; www.galeriaesmoli.net

Icardi
Beautifully understated ceramics, most inspired by ancient designs and fired in their natural colours. Near Cerámica Kinoto (► above), it is marked by a 'Taller de Ceramica' sign.

✉ Just west of Sant Rafel centre, on the main road ☎ 971 19 81 06

Lottie Bogotti
A British-owned boutique on the village high street selling antique and customized jewellery, silks, glassware and eclectica. Hand-cut beads of Bakelite, mother-of-pearl, crystal and other semi-precious stones are used to great effect.

✉ Passatge de les Oliveres, Sant Carles ☎ 618 900 128

MARKETS
See page 69.

ENTERTAINMENT

BARS

Amante

Awesome sea views and a modern Mediterranean menu are the specialities of this stylish, secluded bar-restaurant on the cliffs.

✉ Sol d'en Serra, 1km (0.6 miles) south of Cala Llonga ☎ 971 19 61 76; www.amanteibiza.com 🕐 May–Oct daily 1pm–1am; Nov–Mar Fri–Sun 1pm–1am

Blue Marlin

This slick beach club has put Cala Jondal on the map with great cocktails, banging beats and an achingly fashionable clientele.

✉ Cala Jondal ☎ 971 41 01 17 🕐 May–Oct daily 10am–6am

Café del Mar

The bar that launched Sant Antoni's Sunset Strip and 'chillout' music through DJ José Padilla's sets.

✉ 27 Vara de Rey, Sant Antoni ☎ 971 34 25 16; www.cafedelmarmusic.com 🕐 Mid-Mar to Oct daily noon–4am

Cap d'es Falcó

Turn off at signs en route to Ses Salines and go right past the salt pans to find this chic castaway lounge-bar behind the beach, with a good Italian restaurant – magic at sunset.

✉ Cap d'es Falcó ☎ 971 32 40 82 🕐 Apr–Oct daily 1:30pm–midnight

Las Dalias

This long-running bar is one of northern Ibiza's most celebrated entertainment centres, hosting live rock, jazz and world music and DJ events several nights a week.

✉ At the 12km post on the main road near Sant Carles ☎ 971 33 50 42; www.lasdalias.es

Racó Verd

A highly popular, sociable bar with live music events several nights in summer, and weekly winter events. Jazz, fusion, acoustic and flamenco and rock groups.

✉ Plaça de l'Església, Sant Josep ☎ 971 80 02 67; www.racoverd.es

Zen Sea

With its rattan loungers and spectacular views, this slick beach bar-restaurant brings contemporary sophistication to the area.

✉ Cala Nova, 1km (0.6 miles) north of Es Canar ☎ 971 80 70 26; www.zenseaibiza.com ⏰ Daily 11am–2am

BEST ACTIVITIES

See pages 66–67.

CLUBS

See pages 60–61.

GLASS-BOTTOMED BOATS

There are glass-bottomed boats at several of Ibiza's coves, including Sant Antoni and Port des Torrent. Ask at the tourist office (➤ 29).

GO-KARTS

Fun can be had at the following go-karting circuits.

Sant Antoni ✉ Ctra Eivissa, km 14 ☎ 971 34 38 05 and **Santa Eulària** ✉ On Eivissa road at km 6 marker ☎ 971 31 77 44 ⏰ Both 10am–midnight

GOLF

Club de Golf de Ibiza

✉ On the road from Eivissa to Cala Llonga ☎ 971 19 61 18; www.golfibiza.com

HORSE RACING

Horse racing and pony-trap races can be seen at two venues.

Hippodromo Ibiza ✉ S'Hort Nou, Sant Rafel ☎ 971 19 81 93
Hippodromo Sant Jordi ✉ On the road from Eivissa to the airport, Sant Jordi ☎ 971 30 00 02

MOUNTAIN BIKING

See page 66.

WALKING

See page 67.

Formentera

Swing a map of Formentera about half a turn and squint your eyes, and you can convince yourself that the blueprint for the island was a seahorse. From the straight spine followed by the Via Major, the seahorse's rolled tail follows the eastern coastline from Punta Roja past La Mola to Punta Palmera, while the head points towards Cap de Barbària.

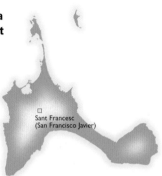

Sant Francesc
(San Francisco Javier)

Many experts believe Formentera's name is derived from the Roman word for a headland, the two headlands of Barbària and La Mola (the head and tail of the seahorse) being such prominent features of an otherwise flat island.

Formentera is a quiet, peaceful place with a hippy vibe, the ideal antidote to the hectic pace of Ibiza. Come here to relax if you have been burning the candle at both ends on the larger island.

CA NA COSTA

In the late 1970s an amateur archaeologist exploring the eastern edge of Estany Pudent (➤ 55), the larger of the two salty lakes to the north of Sant Francesc, discovered the megalithic remains of Ca na Costa. Excavations of the stone circle and nearby grave revealed human remains (including one man who was 2m/6.5ft tall; it's thought he suffered from gigantism), pottery and jewellery, together with axes that date the site to the Bronze Age, around 4,000 years ago.

Ca na Costa is an unusually complex site for its period, and is now recognized as one of the most important sites on the Balearic Islands. It seems likely that Bronze-Age people found a forested island but that their slash-and-burn agriculture destroyed the forests, allowing the fertile top soil to be sun-baked and blown away.

🔁 *Formentera 4d* 🕐 Open access at all times 🍽 Many choices in Es Pujols, including Caminito (€€; ➤ 151, dinner only) 🚌 La Savina–Es Pujols

CALA SAONA

Five kilometres (3 miles) west of Sant Francesc, Cala Saona is a pretty cove beach, its sands and turquoise waters framed by red cliffs and backed by pine trees. There's one large hotel building, but it's set back from the beach and not too obtrusive. Cala Saona is an excellent place to swim and a good starting point for walks to quieter parts of the coast.

Head north for a quiet cliff-top walk, perhaps going as far as Punta de sa Gavina and another well-preserved watchtower, Torre de sa Gavina, built in the late 18th century. Alternatively, head west to Punta Rasa and on to Costa des Bou, where solitude is almost assured.

✛ *Formentera 2c* 🍴 Two *chiringuitos* 🚌 Bus from Sant Francesc

CAP DE BARBÀRIA

The road from Sant Francesc to Cap de Barbària, the southern tip of Formentera, is a good introduction to the landscapes of the island. After leaving the modern buildings of the town behind there are just a few scattered farms – some sheep and goats and the odd cultivated field – but the country soon becomes more arid, scorched by the sun and blown by the wind.

Close to Cap de Barbària (Barbary Cape, named after the pirates), just off the road, are three prehistoric sites, all dating from about 2000BC. Closest to the headland is a stone circle, though the few remaining stones are not easily distinguished from the natural rocks. Next are the remains of several dwellings, the ground plan much more obvious than the stone circle, and finally the remains of another settlement. The sites are protected by fencing, but can easily be seen through the grills.

The empty lighthouse marks the journey's end. Here, as at La Mola (► 42–43), the cliff edge is abrupt and unforgiving. If you stand at the tip of the headland and gaze southwards, the next land, about 220km (137 miles) away, is Africa's northern coast. Head along the eastern edge of the cape to reach Torre des Garroveret, a well-preserved watchtower dating from the mid-18th century. The area around the tower is the preserve of the famous green lizards of Formentera.

✚ *Formentera 2a* ✉ Cap de Barbària is 8km (5 miles) from Sant Francesc 🍴 None 🚌 Not served by buses

S'ESPALMADOR

From Punta de ses Portes, the southern tip of Ibiza, a chain of islets and rocks points the way to Trucadors, the northernmost tip of Formentera. Only one of these islets is big enough to be habitable, or even worth visiting – S'Espalmador, which has the stunning sandy beach of S'Alga.

Trucadors is a curious finger of land, little more than sand dunes dotted with patches of grass and spiky shrubs, and twin beaches that narrow to a point opposite S'Espalmador. The island lies just 200m (220yds) or so from Trucadors' sandy end and you can wade through the sea to it, if conditions are calm. Most visitors, however, choose the less precarious option of a boat ride.

S'Alga beach, occupying the southwestern coast, is the place to head for (though there are no facilities here). From here, a track leads to the northern tip for a view of the nearby islet of Porcs, passing the partially restored watchtower known as Sa Guardiola – the money box.

✠ *Formentera 3f* 🍽 None 🚢 Boats leave La Savina several times daily

ES PUJOLS

Es Pujols is the only resort in
Formentera. Within easy reach of
the village are fine beaches: Platja
des Pujols close to the village, and
those on the low headland of
Trucadors, including Platja de ses
Illetes (➤ 46–47). Facilities on Es
Pujols beach are simpler than on
Ibiza, in keeping with the slower
pace of life on the smaller island.

To the east of the village is the
promontory of Punta Prima. Here
an 18th-century watchtower is
gradually being overshadowed by
tourist hotels. This is the only
place on the island where the
modern development has been
less than sympathetic. However,
with its old fishermen's huts and
a view across Estany Pudent to
Ibiza's southern coast, with Es
Vedrà prominent, Es Pujols is still
an excellent base.

🚩 *Formentera 4d* ✉ On other side
of the Estany Pudent lagoon from La
Savina. Roads circle the lagoon so the
village can be reached either directly
from La Savina, or from Sant Francesc
by way of Sant Ferrán 🍴 Caminito (€€,
➤ 151, dinner only) 🚌 On all routes

LA MOLA

Best places to see, pages 42–43.

LA SAVINA

All ferries between Ibiza and Formentera operate out of La Savina (La Sabina), Formentera's only harbour. It takes its name from the Phoenician word for the juniper which still grows throughout the island. Formentera has no airport, so most visitors' first view of the island is of La Savina, its architecture making it seem more of a North African port than a European one.

Despite its faintly exotic appearance, La Savina is a functioning harbour. It is also the site of one of Formentera's most delightful festivals, Our Lady of the Sea, held annually in July. Then the island's fishing boats gather here before sailing out to be blessed.

La Savina has plenty of rental outlets where cars, bicycles and scooters can be hired to explore the island. From the harbour, Via Major leads inland between the two salty lagoons that are such a notable feature of Formentera.

✚ *Formentera 3d* ✉ Northern coast of the island 🍴 El Tiburón (€€; ► 59) 🚌 On all routes

a walk on Formentera's wild shore

Though this fine walk is a little difficult to follow on occasions, there is ample reward for perseverance.

At the western (Sant Francesc) end of the village of El Pilar de la Mola, the road beside Can Blaiet restaurant heads northwards.

Follow this tarmacked route for about 1.5km (1 mile) to a fork, signed Camí de sa Cala, left. Take this left fork, on a rough track, to a ruined house where a green-and-white sign leads through a makeshift gate and continue alongside a ruined wall. When the wall ends the path soon reaches another wall, low but complete. The cliff-top route is on the other side of this: cross carefully and head across the scrub towards the coast, by guesswork, to reach a vague path occasionally marked with small cairns.
Turn right.

At the cliff edge to the left lies Cova des Fum, the 'Cave of Smoke'. Legend has it that pirates gathered the local Moors here and then killed them by lighting fires that filled the caves with smoke.

The vague path returns to the wall you climbed earlier, which separates a pleasant wood from the cliff. Continue to reach a crossing wall with steps. Head eastwards into woodland then bear left

along a path towards the sea. Go over a wall at a wall junction, head eastwards again and climb a final wall. Continue ahead to reach the cliff edge close to Racó de sa Creu. Now follow a rough path which follows the shallow valley of the Torrent de sa Fontanella, soon reaching a wider track waymarked with arrows and leading back towards El Pilar de la Mola. Pass houses, then follow a more obvious track to reach the road at El Pilar. Turn right to pass the church on the main road at the east end of the village.

Distance 7km (4.5 miles)
Time 3 hours
Start/end point El Pilar de la Mola 🚩 *Formentera 7b*
Lunch El Mirador (€€; ➤ 151) ✉ On main road (Via Major) between Sant Francesc and El Pilar, towards top of long hill ☎ 971 32 70 37

PLATJA DE SES ILLETES
Best places to see, pages 46–47.

PLATJA DE MIGJORN
Forming most of the southern coastline of Formentera, Migjorn is a sweeping sandy beach, interspersed with rocky patches. Extending from the tiny resort area of Es Ca Marí in the west to the base of the La Mola plateau, a distance of around 6km (4 miles), it's large enough for you to be able to find a fairly secluded stretch of sand, even in the busy high season months. There's no

coastal road, so access to the beach is via little tracks (most of them dirt), which extend south from the main inter-island highway.

To get to one of the best sections of beach, take one of these side roads around the km 7 marker on the highway. You'll wind your way through fields of frazzled wheat divided by honey-coloured drystone walls to get to Migjorn. On the beach are some terrific *chiringuitos*, including the Blue Bar and Lucky, where you can take in the enormity of the horizon and feast on fresh seafood.

✚ *Formentera 5b* ✉ South coast of the island 🍴 Blue Bar (€€), Lucky (€)
🚌 Not served by buses except infrequent services to Es Ca Marí

SANT FRANCESC

Sant Francesc (San Francisco Javier) is a complete contrast to Ibiza's capital. It is smaller, with around 1,000 inhabitants, quieter and has a bohemian villagey atmosphere in its historic centre.

In Carrer d'Eivissa, the old chapel – known as Sa Tanca Vell – dates back to the 14th century, though it was carefully restored

in the mid-1980s. The church in the town's main square is an extraordinary building. Erected in the 18th century, it was fortified, as on Ibiza, as a retreat in the event of a pirate attack. But whereas on Ibiza the fortification is rarely at the expense of graceful lines, here it created a bunker seemingly more suited to a nuclear rather than a cutlass attack.

Close by, beside Sa Nostra bank on the pedestrianized Carrer de Jaume I, is the privately owned **Museu Etnològic** (Ethnological Museum), with a collection of traditional island crafts and tools.

✚ *Formentera 3c* ✉ Sant Francesc is Formentera's main town and administrative centre

Museu Etnològic

✉ 17 Carrer de Jaume I ☎ 971 32 26 70 🕐 Mon–Fri 9–2, 5–7 ✋ Inexpensive 🍴 Fonda Platé (€€), Carrer de Santa Maria; Ca Na Pepa (€; ➤ 152) 🚌 La Savina–Es Pujols–Sant Francesc

SES SALINES
Best places to see, pages 54–55.

HOTELS

CAP DE BARBÀRIA
Cap de Barbària (€€€)
A spectacular rural hotel, with very high standards of service, where isolation and tranquillity are guaranteed. Rooms combine rustic architectural features with contemporary styling, and there's a very fine French restaurant (closed Monday).

✉ 5.8km (3.5 miles) south of Sant Francesc ☎ 617 460 629; www.capdebarbaria.com ⏰ Easter–Oct

ES CALÓ
Entrepinos (€€)
On the edge of the La Mola plateau, a short walk from the cove of Es Caló, this hotel, with a pool, makes a comfortable base.

✉ Es Caló ☎ 971 32 70 19; www.hostalentrepinos.com ⏰ May–Oct

ES PUJOLS
Hostal Voramar (€€)
A medium-sized, three-star hotel at the heart of Es Pujols, with pleasant modern(ish) rooms and a pool.

✉ Avinguda Mira Mar ☎ 971 32 81 19; www.hostalvoramar.com ⏰ May–Oct

Roca Bella (€€)
At the north end of the beach, this place feels escapist despite being only 300m (330 yards) from the centre. Sea views in many rooms compensate for dated decor.

✉ Signposted at west entrance of Es Pujols ☎ 971 32 83 61; www.roca-bella.com ⏰ Mid-May to mid-Oct

PLATJA DE MIGJORN
Gecko Beach Club
Refurbished in 2008, this is now a quietly classy getaway whose relaxed minimalist style complements a setting on escapist Platja de Migjorn. All rooms have a terrace, along with garden or sea views.

✉ Es Ca Marí ☎ 971 32 80 24; www.geckobeachclub.com ⏰ May–Oct

LA SAVINA
La Bellavista (€€)
Overlooking the marina, this medium-sized, old-fashioned hotel has large comfortable rooms and a popular café-restaurant.
✉ Plaça de la Marina ☎ 971 32 22 55 🕑 All year

Hostal La Savina (€€)
Rooms are on the small side, but this renovated hotel on the eastern outskirts provides modest, modern style and a beachside location overlooking the lagoon. Pleasant restaurant and bar too.
✉ 22–40 Avinguda Mediterránea ☎ 971 32 22 79; www.hostal-lasavina.com 🕑 May to Oct

RESTAURANTS
ES CALÓ
Can Rafalet (€€)
This restaurant boasts an elegant seafront terrace ideal for a memorable meal and a casual bar area perfect for tapas.
✉ Es Caló ☎ 971 32 70 77 🕑 May–Sep daily 1–4, 8–12

Restaurant Pascual (€€)
Very highly regarded family-run fish restaurant. There's no sea view but the quality of the cooking compensates for this.
✉ Es Caló ☎ 971 32 70 14 🕑 Apr–Oct daily 1–4, 8–12

ES PUJOLS
Caminito (€€)
An Argentinian steak house on the main road near the beach. To find the restaurant, look for the cut-out tango dancers.
✉ Es Pujols ☎ 971 32 81 06 🕑 Daily 8pm–1am

LA MOLA
El Mirador (€€)
The best view on the island, with all but the La Mola headland in sight. The meat and fish dishes are excellent, as is the paella.
✉ Just past the 14km post on Via Major from Sant Francesc to La Mola ☎ 971 32 70 37 🕑 Daily 12–4, 8–12

LA SAVINA
El Tiburón
See page 59.

SANT FERRÁN
Fonda Pepe (€)
This is an old hippy hangout – a bar/restaurant which retains a bohemian atmosphere. Feast on local meats or *arroz a la marinera*.

✉ Sant Ferrán ☎ 971 32 80 33 ◷ Daily 12–12

SANT FRANCESC
Ca Na Pepa (€)
A sedate café-restaurant with a pretty terrace beside the church and a bohemian atmosphere. Serves *bocadillos* (sandwiches) and larger daily specials.

✉ 5 Plaça de la Constitucio ☎ 628 12 20 57 ◷ Easter to mid-Dec Mon–Sat 9:30–3, 8:30–11:30, Sun 10–2

SES ILLETES
Es Molí de Sal (€€€)
One of Formentera's most celebrated restaurants, this place, in a former windmill, has a wonderful outdoor terrace with views over Illetes. The menu includes lobster, paella, barbecued meats and plenty of fresh fish.

✉ Ses Illetes beach ☎ 971 18 74 91 ◷ May–Sep daily 1–4, 8–12

SHOPPING

Can Carlos
An upmarket perfumerie that belies the capital's village looks, Can Carlos sells handmade perfumes blended on the island.

✉ 8 Plaça de la Constitucio, Sant Francesc

Vintage
Modern, flowing women's clothing inspired by bohemian Ad Lib styles, plus beachwear and jewellery handmade on the island. A second outlet is in Es Pujols on Carrer Roca Plana.

✉ 3 Carrer de Santa Maria, Sant Francesc

ENTERTAINMENT

BARS
Blue Bar
The first of the south-coast beach bars and the most faithful to Formentera's laidback bohemian roots. It is at its best at sunset, when crowds gather for drinks, DJs and performers.
✉ Platja de Migjorn (turn off by 8km marker) 🕒 May–early Oct daily 12–12

Flipper&chiller
This chill-out bar sits beside the beach beyond Can Carles. It offers massages, as well as cocktails and Mediterranean cuisine.
✉ Platja de Migjorn (turn off by 11km marker) 🕒 May to mid-Oct noon–1am

CLUB
Xueño (▶ 61)
✉ Es Pujols–Sant Ferrán road 🕒 Jun–Aug

DIVING
Formentera has excellent diving, with wonderful visibility and some wrecks to investigate.
Blue Adventure ✉ 67 Carrer Almadrava, La Savina ☎ 971 32 32 97; www.blue-adventure.com
Vellmarí ✉ 90 Avinguda Mediterránea, La Savina ☎ 971 32 21 05; www.vellmari.com

WALKING
The tourist office (▶ 29) has some excellent leaflets detailing walking routes in Formentera, including the superb Camí Roma, which climbs from Es Caló up to La Mola plateau.

WATER SPORTS
Some of the island's beaches have equipment for hire. The following clubs will help sailors or windsurfers.
Club de Surf Formentera
✉ Es Pujols ☎ 971 32 20 57
Wet Four Fun
✉ Platja des Pujols ☎ 971 32 18 09

Index

Acknowledgements

The Automobile Association would like to thank the following photographers, companies and picture libraries for their assistance in the preparation of this book.

Abbreviations for the picture credits are as follows – (t) top; (b) bottom; (c) centre; (l) left; (r) right; (AA) AA World Travel Library.

4l Platja des Pujols, AA/C Sawyer; **4c** Ferry & Dalt Villa, AA/C Sawyer; **4r** Plaça de Vila, AA/C Sawyer; **5l** Boat excursion, AA/C Sawyer; **5r** Punta Negra from Sa Talaia, AA/C Sawyer; **6/7** Platja de Pujols, AA/C Sawyer; **8/9** Market stall, AA/C Sawyer; **10/11t** Drystone wall, AA/C Sawyer; **10c** Michaelmas daisies, AA/J Tims; **10bl** Cala Llonga, AA/C Sawyer; **10br** Pottery, AA/C Sawyer; **11c** Traditional costume, AA/C Sawyer; **11b** Almond and fig trees, AA/C Sawyer; **12/13** Market stall, La Marina, AA/C Sawyer; **12** Paella, AA/C Sawyer; **13c** Bullit de peix, AA/C Sawyer; **13b** Buillit de peix, AA/C Sawyer; **14t** Cafés, Plaça de Vila, AA/C Sawyer; **14b** Coffee and ensaimada, AA/C Sawyer; **15t** Flao cake, AA/C Sawyer; **15c** Sangria bottles, AA/C Sawyer; **15b** Hierbas bottles, AA/C Sawyer; **16** Fashion boutique, AA/C Sawyer; **17** Sangria, AA/C Sawyer; **16/17** La Marina harbour, AA/J Tims; **18/19** Shoppers, La Marina, AA/C Sawyer; **19t** Tour boat, Cala Llonga, AA/C Sawyer; **19b** Cap de Barbaria, AA/C Sawyer; **20/21** Harbour, Eivissa, AA/C Sawyer; **24** Traditional dancing, AA/C Sawyer; **25** Eivissa, Festival of Sant Ciriac, Pictures Colour Library; **26** Ferry terminal, Sant Antoni de Portmany, AA/C Sawyer; **27** Bus station, Sant Antoni de Portmany, AA/C Sawyer; **31** Telephone box, AA/C Sawyer; **32** Policeman, AA/J Tims; **34/35** Plaça de Vila, AA/C Sawyer; **36** Beach bar, Cala d'Hort, AA/C Sawyer; **37** Cala d'Hort, AA/C Sawyer; **38/39t** Cathedral Museum, AA/C Sawyer; **38/39b** Cathedral Museum, AA/C Sawyer; **39** Altarpiece, Dalt Vila Cathedral, AA/C Sawyer; **40t** Isodor Macabich, Plaça des Desamparats, AA/C Sawyer; **40b** Cafés, Plaça de Vila, AA/C Sawyer; **40/41** Street scene, Dalt Vila, AA/C Sawyer; **42** Cap de la Mola, Formentera, AA/C Sawyer; **43** Windmill, Formentera, AA/C Sawyer; **44** Jesús Church, AA/C Sawyer; **44/45** Altar screen, Jesús Church, AA/C Sawyer; **46/47** Platja de ses Illetes, AA/C Sawyer; **48** Platja de ses Salines, AA/C Sawyer; **49** Platja de ses Salines, AA/C Sawyer; **50** Café, Santa Eulària des Riu, AA/C Sawyer; **50/51** Fountain, Santa Eulària des Riu, AA/C Sawyer; **51** Harbour, Santa Eulària des Riu, AA/C Sawyer; **52/53** Can Daifa Gallery, Santa Gertrudis, AA/C Sawyer; **53** Shops, Santa Gertrudis, AA/C Sawyer; **54/55** Salt lagoon, Formentera, AA/C Sawyer; **56/57** Boat excursion, AA/C Sawyer; **58/59** Café/bar, Cala Mastella, AA/C Sawyer; **60/61** Sant Antoni de Portmany, AA/C Sawyer; **62/63** Talamanca beach, AA/C Sawyer; **64** Watchtower, Punta des Portes, AA/C Sawyer; **65** Platja des Cavellet, AA/C Sawyer; **67** Platja de ses Salinas, AA/C Sawyer; **68** Punta Arabí Hippy Market, AA/C Sawyer; **69** Jewellery, market stall, AA/C Sawyer; **70/71** View out to sea from Baluard de Sant Bernat, AA/J Tims; **72/73** Punta Negra from Sa Talaia, AA/C Sawyer; **75** Ceremonial ramp and Portal de ses Taules, AA/J Tims; **76/77** Cathedral and Old Town, Eivissa, AA/C Sawyer; **77** Episcopal palace, Eivissa, AA/C Sawyer; **78** Cafés, La Marina, Eivissa, AA/C Sawyer; **80** Portal de ses Taules, AA/C Sawyer; **81** Views from Plaça de la Catedral, Eivissa, AA/C Sawyer; **82** Statue of Joaquim Vara de Rey, Eivissa, AA/C Sawyer; **82/83** Town Hall, Eivissa, AA/C Sawyer; **84** Roman statue, Eivissa, AA/C Sawyer; **84/85** Necropolis of Puig des Molins, AA/C Sawyer; **86** Sa Penya, AA/C Sawyer; **87** Sa Penya, AA/C Sawyer; **88t** Altar, Sant Domènec Church, AA/C Sawyer; **88b** Dome, Sant Domènec Church, AA/J Tims; **121b** Market stall, Sant Josep, AA/C Sawyer; **95** Cala Xarraca, AA/C Sawyer; **96** Defence tower, Balàfia, AA/C Sawyer; **97** Cala Llonga, AA/C Sawyer; **98/99** Cala Salada, AA/C Sawyer; **100** Marina, Es Canar, AA/C Sawyer; **100/101** Es Cubells, AA/C Sawyer; **102** Roman bridge, Santa Eulària des Riu, AA/C Sawyer; **103** Town Hall, Sant Joan De Labritja, AA/C Sawyer; **104/105** View of Es Vedra and Es Vedranell, AA/C Sawyer; **106/107** Hotel Hacienda Na Xamena, AA/C Sawyer; **107** Cova de Can Marca, AA/C Sawyer; **108/109** Port des Torrent, AA/C Sawyer; **110/111** Cala Portinatx, AA/C Sawyer; **111** Museu Etnològic d'Eivissa i Formentera, AA/C Sawyer; **112/113** Punta Arabí Hippy Market, AA/C Sawyer; **114/115** Sa Caleta, AA/C Sawyer; **115** Agnus Dei statue, Santa Agnès de Corona, AA/C Sawyer; **116/117** Harbour, Sant Antoni de Portmany, AA/C Sawyer; **117** Cova de ses Llegostes Aquarium, AA/C Sawyer; **118** 'Stations of the Cross', Sant Carles de Peralta church, AA/C Sawyer; **118/119** Sant Carles de Peralta church, AA/C Sawyer; **120** Sculpture, Sant Joan de Labritja Church, AA/C Sawyer; **121t** Bell tower, Sant Josep, AA/J Tims; **121b** Market stall, Sant Josep, AA/C Sawyer; **122/123** Folk costume, Sant Miquel de Balansat, AA/C Sawyer; **123** Benirràs painting, Sant Miquel de Balansat chapel, AA/C Sawyer; **124/125** Serra Grossa, AA/J Tims; **126/127** Talamanca beach, AA/C Sawyer; **137** Platja des Pujols, AA/C Sawyer; **138/139** Ca na Costa, AA/C Sawyer; **139** Cala Saona, AA/C Sawyer; **140/141** Cap de Barbaria, AA/C Sawyer; **142/143** Harbour, La Savina, AA/C Sawyer; **144** Lizard, Formentera, AA/C Sawyer; **144/145** El Pilar de la Mola church, AA/C Sawyer; **146/147** Platja Migjorn, AA/C Sawyer; **148/149** Sant Francesc church, AA/C Sawyer; **149** Ethnological museum, Sant Francesc, AA/C Sawyer.

Every effort has been made to trace the copyright holders, and we apologise in advance for any accidental errors. We would be happy to apply the corrections in the following edition of this publication.

Sight locator index

This index relates to the maps on the covers. We have given map references to the main sights in the book. Grid references in italics indicate sights featured on the town plan and the Formentera map. Some sights within towns may not be plotted on the maps.

Dear Reader

Your comments, opinions and recommendations are very important to us. Please help us to improve our travel guides by taking a few minutes to complete this simple questionnaire.

You do not need a stamp (unless posted outside the UK). If you do not want to cut this page from your guide, then photocopy it or write your answers on a plain sheet of paper.

Send to: **The Editor, AA World Travel Guides,
FREEPOST SCE 4598, Basingstoke RG21 4GY.**

Your recommendations...

We always encourage readers' recommendations for restaurants, nightlife or shopping – if your recommendation is used in the next edition of the guide, we will send you a **FREE AA Guide** of your choice from this series. Please state below the establishment name, location and your reasons for recommending it.

_____
_____
_____
_____
_____

Please send me **AA Guide** _____

About this guide...

Which title did you buy?

AA _____

Where did you buy it? _____

When? **m m** / **y y**

Why did you choose this guide? _____
_____
_____
_____

Did this guide meet your expectations?

Exceeded ☐ Met all ☐ Met most ☐ Fell below ☐

Were there any aspects of this guide that you particularly liked? _____
_____
_____
_____

continued on next page...

Is there anything we could have done better? _____

_____

_____

_____

About you...

Name (*Mr/Mrs/Ms*) _____

Address _____

_____

_____ Postcode _____

Daytime tel nos _____

Email _____

Please only give us your mobile phone number or email if you wish to hear from us about
other products and services from the AA and partners by text or mms, or email.

Which age group are you in?
Under 25 ☐   25–34 ☐   35–44 ☐   45–54 ☐   55–64 ☐   65+ ☐

How many trips do you make a year?
Less than one ☐   One ☐   Two ☐   Three or more ☐

Are you an AA member? Yes ☐   No ☐

About your trip...

When did you book? m m / y y   When did you travel? m m / y y

How long did you stay? _____

Was it for business or leisure? _____

Did you buy any other travel guides for your trip? _____

If yes, which ones? _____

_____

_____

Thank you for taking the time to complete this questionnaire. Please send it to us as soon as
possible, and remember, you do not need a stamp (*unless posted outside the UK*).

AA Travel Insurance call 0800 072 4168 or visit www.theAA.com

---